I0101427

The Nice Guy's Guide To Online Dating Profiles

Buffy Greentree

Copyright © 2014 Buffy Greentree

All rights reserved.

Published by The Buffy Group

ISBN-13: 9780992356118

To my Dad, he got his girl in the end.

Table of Content

ABOUT THE AUTHOR

Evelyn: Look, I... I may not be an explorer, or an adventurer, or a treasure-seeker, or a gunfighter, Mr. O'Connell, but I am proud of what I am.
Rick: And what is that?
Evelyn: I... am a librarian.

Evelyn Carnahan, *The Mummy* (1999)

So who am I?

Well I'm not a librarian, sorry for any false fantasies you were developing. But like Evelyn, I'm proud of what I am. And what is that? I'm a writer! (And an entrepreneur, but the writer part is way cooler.)

As well as running a boutique company providing self-publishing services and consultancy, I also write both fiction and non-fiction. What do I write exactly? Well, I'll give most things a go at least once (note that I said most things. Keep your mind out of the gutter, please). I also maintain three blogs on writing, fitness and theology. You can check it all out at www.thebuffygroup.com, the HQ to my evil empire.

My first degree started off as a Bachelor of Arts majoring in Psychology. Unfortunately I got midway through third year and realised that I didn't want to be a psychologist and instead majored in Classics and Archaeology. I then went on to do a few other degrees, all up spending a decade in academia, before getting a real job, quitting it and becoming a writer and building my company. That's the cliff notes version.

The basic result of my career choices is that I have a broad range of knowledge in a number of fields, and I now spend a lot of time behind a computer not meeting many people. Because of this latter issue, internet dating made a whole lot of sense.

So, why am I writing this book?

Well, I've always had a soft spot for the underdog, but not a strong desire to date them.

While going through the online dating circus, there were a number of times I just had to say 'I'm sorry, I'm not interested, but do you want some tips on how to improve your profile?' To my surprise, this offer was always accepted. One guy was so eager for help that he immediately emailed me his login and password.

My father was a nice but nerdy guy in his day, and stuffed up so badly while dating my mother that it took another two years before she finally agreed to go on a third date. Because of his experiences, he has always told me that I should give the nice but geeky guys a fair go. He would argue that it's not their fault that they come across so badly. My dad is fantastic, and obviously, nerdy guys can make great life partners. However, wouldn't it be easier for everyone involved if they came across just a little bit better to begin with?

So for the sake of my dad, and other future generations of children who could be like me, I am now providing my suggestions to the world of nice guys out there. I'm not going to turn you into something you're not, but I will show you how you can come up shinning.

You know you want to win my heart.

PART ONE

INTRODUCTION

WELCOME

Welcome to *The Nice Guy's Guide To Online Dating Profiles*. Just to clarify, this is a guide for nice guys who want to write a more effective online dating profile, not a guide written by nice guys. It was written by me, Buffy Greentree. Yup, that's my photo. You know, a quiet Saturday night in. And yes, at the time of writing this I am single and for the past year I've been doing the online dating thing, which has resulted in a lot of fun dates with nice guys (and one or two disasters with complete creeps, so if any of them are reading this... this book isn't for you, because it's for nice guys). Because of my area of expertise, it is obviously aimed at guys who are looking for girls, and generally girls something like me. (I would like to think that nice guys looking for other nice guys would at least have some advantage over their heterosexual counterparts, not having to guess what women want.) So, if you think of yourself as a nice guy, and honestly want the whole relationship thing to work, then this book will help.

Sadly, the advice in this book is so good that even if you are not a nice guy it will probably help improve your dating chances, but only until the point you have to meet in person and they realise you are a sleaze. That's on you, my friend. So I'm ignoring you if you're reading this book for nefarious purposes, and take no responsibility for how things work out. But for everyone else, welcome and take a seat.

So here you are, for whatever reason – a sudden dumping, moving cities, realising you are getting old – you have decided to try internet dating. Well done. It is a brave first step, and opens up a world of opportunities, even if love isn't immediately apparent. But with just a bit of help you can make this endeavour a whole lot more fun for everyone involved. In order to help you succeed, we are going to call on three distinct disciplines: psychology (so we can get inside everyone's heads), internet marketing (to create a selling brand), and writing (to polish your words to perfection).

Now stop.

Yes, I know you are excited, and you want to jump online and start searching for girls. We will get to that in a moment. Like taking any action, failure to plan is planning to fail!

When you sign up to a dating site, you are going to be asked to make a whole lot of decisions, some of which cannot be undone without closing your profile and starting all over again. (If you have already created a poor profile and can't get out of it, I do recommend closing down and trying somewhere else for a while. Brand new starts are always exciting.) You don't want to rush into making these decisions without a game plan, because each of these decisions will reflect on you for better or worse. So we are going to take some time developing your strategy first.

The basic outline of this book is pretty simple. It's divided into three sections which should be done in order. In each part there are steps to take you further along the road to working out exactly what it is you want and then creating an engaging profile to get it. The former is just as important as the latter, but strangely often overlooked.

So after doing a bit of preparation to ensure you are really making the best move, we start with the psychology of online dating. Having done a sub-major in psychology in my bachelor's degree, I've ignored all the pop psychology and gone straight to the hardcore academic articles (there's a bibliography at the end to prove it!). These guys know more about why you do things than you do. With their help we are going to crack the 'what women want' riddle and give you an edge in creating a killer profile while avoiding any red flags. Psychology will also reassure you that this isn't as crazy a move as you might think.

Next we move onto the internet marketing section. I am not an internet marketer myself, you may be relieved to know, but have studied its principles from a branding perspective. They are *the* guys on how to sell yourself online and attract attention, which is pretty much what we are trying to achieve. Along with looking at your own branding, we will also look at who you are trying to attract. Internet marketing is all about finding and appealing to your target audience. By the time you finish this section, you will have a solid strategy on where to go, who to look for, and how to present yourself.

In the final section, my personal favourite, we are going to use the craft of good storytelling (which as Stephen King says in his book *On Writing*, is all about telling the truth) to actually write each of the different elements required in a profile. By using the techniques of the best writers, we will make sure you have an accurate and enticing face for the online world. Sound good? Great, let's get stuck in.

Are You Ready For This?

Let's start at the very beginning. How important is having a partner to you right now? This is not a question of how desperate you are, but one of your priorities. How does it fit in with where you are now and what you are working towards in other areas of your life? Is owning your own home, having a great career, being super fit and healthy more or less important? All because you have picked up/been given a book on internet dating, doesn't mean that now is the best time for you to focus on this. As your first practical step towards online dating, I want you to work out if you actually want to dedicate the time and effort needed in order to achieve a satisfactory outcome. I'm going to get you to do an exercise from Tim Ferris' *4-*

Hour Work Week, so you can see more clearly what is most important to you at the moment. You will need pen and paper, or an open text document. Ready?

Okay, picture your ideal future just 12 months from now.

Don't restrict yourself in anyway, be as completely ridiculous as you like. Imagine it fully in your mind, where you are, what you have, what you're doing.

Right, now take a few minutes to list out five things that you see in this future under each the following headings (fifteen in total):

1. Having.
2. Being.
3. Doing.

For example, you might list:

1. Having:
House by the beach
Beautiful girlfriend
…

2. Being:
Fluent in French
Strong enough to do 100 push-ups
…

3. Doing:
Running your own business

Travelling in South America

...

Be as outrageous as you can, and list five things under each in any particular order. Don't hold back, and make sure that you have the full five before going on. Let your imagination run wild and see what makes you feel most content or excited.

Finished? Really?

Okay, out of those fifteen items, I want you to pick your top four. I want you to choose the four things that would make the biggest difference to your life right now if you achieved them. They don't have to be the most realistic, or even the hardest to achieve. But if you could make four things happen in your life by the end of 12 months, which would be the most life changing for you?

Thought all that through?

Is finding a partner one of them? Would finding a partner in the next 12 months be one of the biggest positive changes you could make in your life? Similarly, if you achieved any of the rest of your goals, would it change where, how and who you were looking for?

If the answer to the first question is no, that's not a problem. It doesn't mean that it's not important to you in general, but I would recommend at the moment that you put your energy into achieving those four things, because if you did, you might find that what you were looking for in a partner would also change. Furthermore, you only have certain amounts of time and energy, and it would be more sensible to direct these towards the things that will make the biggest difference in your life. For you, I recommend putting down this book here, and starting to work out how you can achieve these four things. Or even better, give this book to someone else you think it might help, but remind them to give it back to you in 12 months' time.

For those who want to prioritise finding a partner, but also think that if you achieved your other goals what you would be looking for would be different, I suggest you wait. Give yourself a set period of time to focus on achieving your other goals. If you don't do it by then, come back to this book and pick up where you left off. If you do, come back to this book and we'll create a strategy based on your new situation.

Now, for everyone who answered yes to the first question, welcome. You have decided that putting in the time and energy to find a partner is worth it, because this would make a substantial difference to your life. This is great.

So, just to be clear, how much time and effort were you planning on putting in? You have said that this is one of your top priorities, therefore I expect you to be prepared to put in a significant amount of effort to learn how to best achieve your goal, and then actually work towards it. No more hoping it will happen by chance, or hoping a slap-dash effort will get you the results you want. This is going to take strategic thought and planning, as it should.

So, Lone Star, now you see that evil will always triumph because good is dumb.

Dark Helmet, *Spaceballs* (1987).

The truth is that nice guys often finish last because they do not prioritise what they want. In the words of Dark Helmet, they are dumb. Guys who want to be 'players' put a lot of time and effort into learning how to present themselves and attract women, but for all the wrong reasons! Most online profiles of nice guys are put together in less than 20 minutes, often state things like 'umm, I'm just trying this out' or 'I don't really know what to say about myself'. Does that reflect to potential partners how much importance you place on this? For all women out there I command you to at least equal the effort of players, because we need more smart, good guys out there.

So, it is time for you to take control and master this field.

PART TWO

THE PSYCHOLOGY OF IT ALL

CHAPTER ONE

REPRESENTING YOURSELF

The Psychology of Internet Dating

We are going to start with the basics and build from there to make sure you fully understand what you are doing and how you can do it better. The first step is to understand how you present yourself and how computers change all that.

All dating involves finding the best possible way to communicate what we consider as our 'self' in a way that is attractive and also honest because we want to be truly understood. Simple, right? Um, yeah, maybe not. There are two problems with this. The first is knowing what to communicate, and the second is knowing how best to communicate it so it is correctly received. We all know that when put on the spot, it is difficult to summarise yourself, so we are going to spend a lot of time on this later. But the theory behind how we communicate is equally important in order to be successful. In normal face to face interaction, we are constantly trying to show other people (or hide) who we think we are. No need to feel ashamed, everyone does it, some people just do it more successfully than others. However, this is only part of the equation.

According to Goffman's theory, people build an image of us using the unintentional cues we give off as much as what we verbally say about ourselves. For example, meeting a beautiful woman, you might believe (and try to make her believe) that you are calm and confident. However, at the same time your shoulders are tight and you are moving from one foot to the other. This is not a good match up. The woman is more likely to believe what you are subconsciously doing, and the disparateness between the two is going to reflect badly on you. If you really want to succeed in this game, you need to know and understand these unintentional cues, because people who have a coherent message between the two are better received. It comes across as being honest and self-aware, very attractive characteristics.

So you need to know how to use both intentional and unintentional cues to support your message. This applies to all areas of life, but particularly in trying to impress a mate. We need to make sure that everything is working together to send out the same message, and that we know what that message is! However, being online really mixes things up.

The Advantages

Most nice guys I know who are unsuccessful in real life dating can blame it on their unintentional cues, which usually come from anxiety and uncertainty about how they should be presenting themselves. If you feel this might be true of you, even to a small extent, then online dating gives you an advantage, if you use it correctly.

Online dating is great because it gives you more control over how and when you portray yourself. Have you ever become a stammering fool when introduced to the new girl at work? Or had a comment slip out that you knew was stupid the moment you said it? Internet dating is the simple yet effective way to overcome these problems. As early as 1992, Walther noticed that 'computer-mediated communication', aka chatting online, allowed people the time to think about how they wanted to best present themselves, as well as being able to edit and take back things that came out wrong. So if you are just a little shy, embrace what the internet has to offer.

Furthermore, taking more time to think about how you want to respond and 'selectively self-represent' doesn't make the communication any less honest. A group led by Knox in 2001 found that because people could relax and were less self-conscious online, their true self was more likely to emerge. If you have ever walked away from a meeting slapping your head because you came across like a complete idiot, this is good news.

19

Steve: *Well, how'd it go?*

Jeff: *She's leaving the country, she doesn't speak English, I insulted her friend's breasts and she thinks I collect women's ears in a bucket.*

Steve: *Well, you've had worse.*

"The Girl With Two Breasts," *Coupling*, Season 1
Episode 5, (2000)

The Disadvantages

One of the great advantages of being online is that it is much easier to monitor what you are presenting to the world. There are fewer things to concentrate on, so it is easier to give a unified message. You don't have to worry about what your hands are doing, an impending bodily noise, or whether you are wearing mismatched socks. This is all great. However, there are two distinct disadvantages that arise from having less cues from the other person.

The first is that people like being able to compare the unintentional cues with the intentional ones to make sure everything lines up. Online, while there are less cues, this does not mean that people don't pay attention to anything other than the stated message. Just the opposite. Because there are only a few cues available, these suddenly take on a lot more meaning than they might otherwise. As Fiore, *et al.* (2008) state, 'everything from the username (or "handle") to the use of language or the choice of a photograph can signal certain qualities in online interaction; some signals "give" intended meaning while simultaneously "giving off" additional unintended information.' This means that you have to be very careful about every aspect of your online profile, to make sure it isn't giving off messages that undermine what you are trying to say. You need to understand what possible 'red flags' you could be raising.

If you are not having luck online, don't take it personally. The most likely reason is that other people are reading things into your profile that you didn't know were there. But never fear: that is why you have this book. As we go through each aspect of the profile, I'll highlight how things can be misinterpreted and what you can do to make all cues as positive as possible.

The second major disadvantage is that because of the paucity of cues, and the opportunity for selective self-representation, most people are worried that others aren't telling the truth.

Truthfulness Online

Are you, or maybe some of your friends and family, sceptical about being online because everyone can lie? You're not the only ones. Strangely, as mentioned, being online can give you the opportunity to be more honest and self-revealing, but most people don't see it this way. Everyone thinks that other people are lying, but research has found that in fact, in an online dating situation where the ultimate goal is to meet face to face, people tend to be more truthful. There is a deep need in everyone to have their true self known, and as such there are conscious and unconscious desires to be truthful when searching for a partner. Therefore, while some lying does happen, generally in smaller and predictable ways, Ellison, *et al.* (2006) argue that 'our interview data suggest that the notion that people frequently, explicitly and intentionally "lie" online is simplistic and inaccurate.' This is supported by Joinson (2001) who found that under certain conditions, online communication allowed the user to express themselves more openly and honestly than they would otherwise.

So why does everyone think everyone else is lying? This fear comes from the inability to verify the information we receive. We are made to read the intentional and unintentional signals everyone gives off, usually in abundance. Take most of those away and we become fearful, thinking we have to rely on just what people tell us, which we know from experience can often be shown false by other cues. So while in fact online dating is generally quite truthful, there are things you can do to make people feel more secure and perceive you as more honest.

The big question now is how to make your profile appear honest. Well, surprisingly, it is not by spilling all your dark secrets (this is unsettling for the reader as it breaks social norms about self-disclosure, so please don't do it). Instead, 'honest' profiles usually use as many of the additional cues available to support the information stated. Imagine you are reading two different profiles. Both say that they are 'active, outgoing and down to earth'. One has the handle 'FitandFun', then includes a photograph of them running a triathlon, as well as using energetic words for their self-description, and finishing with a description of their favourite Friday night hanging out at the rock-climbing gym. The other one has the name '83hgbs' (no joke, people use random collections of letters and numbers, more on this later), has just one picture of a pug dog (no person in sight), and a badly spelt profile saying they are looking for love. In this second profile, there is nothing that suggests either way if they are telling the truth, but generally people will vote the first one much more honest, and therefore appealing.

This is good news for you, as we are going in depth into how you can use this.

In Conclusion

For those who like to skim chapters, here are the major points from this section:

1. Everyone, in every context, is always constructing how to present themselves.

2. If you do not feel other people view you as you view yourself, it is usually because of the unintentional signals you are giving off, in life as well as online.

3. Online communication can allow you to overcome many of your difficulties, but it can also

exaggerate them if you don't take time to look at what you are saying from another's perspective.

4. Don't go in with the attitude that everyone is lying.

5. Be optimistic about this journey. Going in with a pessimistic attitude is a complete turn off for other people. Just saying.

CHAPTER TWO

WHAT WOMEN WANT

Don't Start With The Wrong Idea

Many people come into online dating with such a negative attitude that it reflects in their profiles, interactions and consequently their success. Particularly those men who come with preconceived ideas about 'what women want', in a negative sense, often shoot themselves in the foot. Two of the most common complaints I've heard are: 'girls only want hot guys' and 'they are only interested in the photo'. So before we start crafting your online profile, let's take a moment to see what psychological studies have found about how women act online. You don't have to take just my word for it.

Psychology has also been trying to work out what women want. Foire and Donath (2005) focused on what women considered 'attractive' in an online profile. What they found was that it wasn't if the men were good looking. Rather, women were more attracted to older more educated men with higher levels of self-confidence. Clearly, women do not just want hot guys.

And it's not just the photograph that makes for an attractive profile, according to Foire, *et al.* (2008). For a profile to be judged as above average in attractiveness, it needed an appealing self-summary along with a photo. They argue that 'this first set of analysis points to the importance of having both an attractive photo and an attractive free-text component in order to have an attractive profile.'

And the real secret about what women really want in a mate? Honey, it's all relative.

To work out what people were really looking for (not just what they said), Hitsch, *et al.* (2010) followed the choices of thousands of online daters. From this they made a list of what most women preferred in different categories.

Age: Women prefer men who are their age or up to 9 years older. Young was less preferred, and anything 10+ years younger or older was even less preferred.

Looks: While both men and women preferred better-looking partners, men have a much stronger preference about looks than women. (So there – who's saying women were the ones wanting hot partners?)

Weight: Women had a very different preference regarding weight than men in that they preferred partners with a higher BMI (Body Mass Index) than their own, but disliked men with a lower BMI. However, again men have a much stronger preference about weight than women.

(And you wonder why we are self-conscious about our weight!)

Height: There was no preference about absolute heights of potential partners, it was all relative. Women preferred men who were taller than them, and were not interested in men shorter. (So short men, you don't have to despair, you just need to find someone shorter than yourself.)

Income: Unlike height, income preference was on an absolute level, not a relative one. Both men and women preferred a high-income partner over a low-income one, though this preference is stronger in women. The largest increase in being contacted was in the $50k – $75k range, and smaller increases from then on.

Education: Interestingly, both men and women showed a preference for partners with a similar level of education, regardless of what that level was.

Occupation: This had a strong influence on women's preferences. Using 'student' as a baseline, the study found that the top four occupations were 'Legal/Attorney', then 'Law Enforcement/Fire fighter', then 'Military' and finally the health professions. Obviously it's not just about your pay packet, though a uniform appears to help.

Race: While it might feel politically incorrect to say, in both men and women there was a same-race preference, though it was more pronounced in women.

Similarity: Finally, in other aspects such as marital status, type of relationship goals, smoking etc., there was a preference for similarity. If the woman was a smoker, she preferred smokers, etc.

Based on this evidence, it is very difficult to say 'all women want...' because a lot of it is relative to their situation. So you first need to work out who your ideal woman is to find out if you might be her ideal man and how to show her this.

CHAPTER THREE

DESCRIBING YOURSELF

Who Are You?

For the final section on psychology, I thought it was appropriate to do a bit of self-examination. It is psychology, after all. The aim is to get a better grasp on who you really are; both who you think you are and how you come across. Let's start with who you think you are.

Anyone who has tried to write a self-summary will understand that we rarely think of ourselves as a unified concept. There are so many different aspects, and we show these differently depending in the relationship and circumstances; there are parts that we don't want to admit, other parts we don't really think about, and all that stuff in the middle. This makes trying to get anything down on paper very difficult. So when we are forced to come up with something, there are some dangers that can occur.

Here is something to consider. According to Higgins (1987) we think of ourselves in three ways: the *actual self* (the attributes we possess), the *ideal self* (the attributes we would like to possess), and the *ought self* (attributes we feel we ought to possess). Often when writing online profiles, people are tempted to describe a potential or ideal version of self. I found this a lot with guys who obviously described themselves as they wanted to be, but it conflicted with a lot of the other cues they were giving off. A common example I came across was that they would say they went to the gym frequently, but their picture suggested that at best it was quite a while ago. While it's not exactly lying, the conflicting cues make the reader uncomfortable. Basically, you could be turning people off contacting you. So we need to work out who you really are at the moment, and not fall into the ideal/ought self trap.

We are about to enter into some self-examination, which should be undertaken with extreme caution, as it can have awful effects on self-esteem if not handled properly. So, first I want you to go and get dressed up. Put on your favourite Hawaiian shirt, or the hat you won for drinking ten margaritas. Anything that makes you feel comfortable and positive. Now make yourself a playlist of music that brings a smile to your face, and grab a beer or alcoholic drink of choice (but only one or two, I still need you to be able to write).

Feeling better?

Good, now sit back and relax, it's time for some soul searching.

Your Attributes

On a scrap piece of paper I want you to start listing your attributes. Start by focusing on all the positive ones. Lots and lots of positive ones. Unfortunately, being a 'nice guy' should not be one of them. This is not actually a real attribute. It is generally expected that most people do try to be nice. Rather, you need to think like an advertiser: what are your unique selling points and value propositions? If you were a girl, why would you want to date you?

This is a time to be honest and not beat yourself up. Sinking into depression and declaring that no one will ever love you is not the aim of the game. You have your lucky hat on, you're grooving to the beat, and the alcohol is starting to take away some of your inhibitions (please just promise me that you won't post your profile before reading it in the cold light of day).

What have you always been secretly (or not so secretly) proud of?

Assuming that no one will ever read this piece of paper, write down absolutely everything you like about yourself. Everything, even if it is that you have nicely shaped nails. This is not a time to hold back. Throw caution to the wind and write down that you are an expert at beating the computer at chess, when set on easy.

Now, I don't want adjectives, I want you to give me examples. This is the way to make sure it is an actual attribute, not just an ideal one. Further, it helps you in the writing section if you have actual examples. You say you're friendly? How do you know? Do dogs always come up with their tails wagging? Did you go and introduce yourself to all the wallflowers at your mother's last Christmas party? Give me proof!

I want you to spend at least an hour wracking your brain. Yup, a whole hour. Don't get up until the timer has run out. Don't stop at the first ten ideas, the first ten ideas are always the lamest. Keep going, dig deeper, find more golden nuggets.

Right, starting to run out of ideas?

Okay, now for the harder bit: we are going to look at some negatives. If you need help, start by listing five attributes you just don't have. As a personal example, I really cannot sing. Would love to, and have a special pocketful of jealousy for girls who can, but it's not a talent I possess (not that I let it stop me at karaoke). If it is really important to a guy that he has a musically gifted girlfriend to sing in his band, I might as well keep moving. This is not selling myself short, it's about finding a better match and saving everyone some time.

So what are your negatives?

There are a few other good reasons for doing this:

1. Being self-aware is its own reward.

2. If you realise you have an annoying habit that could put off the perfect partner, you might try to overcome it.

3. Profiles that mix in a few funny negatives can get away with a lot more boasting.

4. It will help you find your 'niche' partner more easily.

So don't avoid this step, or be too superficial about it. It could be very enlightening.

Keep writing and don't go onto the next section until you have loads of positives and a few negatives. But when you feel ready, it's time to see how other people view you.

External Representation

You have just taken a very long time (hopefully) to list out how you perceive yourself. As you've peppered it with examples and evidence, this should be reasonably accurate. However, we all have our blind spots. These could be faults we just don't want to admit, or they could be golden qualities we think aren't that special. However, when writing a profile, it's important that we know how our messages and previous self representation efforts have been interpreted. Basically, to write a good profile you need to develop some self-awareness of how others see you. As a happy side note, if you have a close match between your own self-perception and how others perceive you then you are a much more psychologically healthy person. Isn't that nice to know? Now is a great time to find out if this is something you could work on to make you more satisfied with life.

So, let's start with the small stuff that doesn't require you to put yourself out there just yet.

What was the nicest compliment you ever received, even if you didn't believe it?

Try to write down a list of all the compliments you have received in the last week/month/year.

Now the reverse side, what criticisms have you received lately? Don't be harsh on yourself, just list what people might have said (though you can leave out anyone you know to be an utter jerk who says incorrect things about everyone).

Now we are moving onto the big stuff. I would highly, highly recommend not skipping this step. Highly. Very, very highly. Got it? Right.

It's time to get your friends and family involved, the people who you interact with the most. It is time to find out what they really think about you. (By the way, if you are at all scared about what your friends might say, then you might need to think about getting new friends. If you don't think they are going to be generally encouraging with just one or two truths to hit home, then I would recommend clearing them out of your life before you start bringing in someone special. You don't want your perfect woman to have to put up with jerks, do you?)

Instead of talking to each of them, which will put awkward pressure on both of you, and not necessarily give us the results we want, we are going to rely on an anonymous survey. This will take a bit longer to set up and then wait for all the results, but it is a fantastic life lesson that I think everyone should do at least once, regardless of whether you are writing a profile.

An Independent Audit

My first recommendation would be to use the Independent Audit offered through the 'Winner's Bible' Website. (*The Winner's Bible* might also be a book you could think about reading. I read it a number of years ago, so can't remember everything, but remember that it was helpful at the time. As you are already on the path to make changes in your life, why not look at other ways and areas as well?)

The audit works like this:

You invite a minimum of four people to provide feedback about you – there is no maximum. These are your 'auditors'.

Each auditor then writes a series of short paragraphs about you in a special confidential part of the Winner's Bible website. Each paragraph should be a self-contained thought about you along with any suggestions corresponding to that thought. They can go back and edit/change/delete their comments until your audit is closed, at least 10 days after you start.

You don't get to see any comments about you until:

a) You close your audit after a minimum of 10 days,

b) At least four people have written comments about you,

c) 24 hours passed after you closed your audit.

Then and only then are the comments from all the auditors shuffled and combined in a way so you don't know who wrote which comment about you.

This survey focuses on your strengths and weaknesses and might help you to see patterns you couldn't see by yourself. Though, fair warning, you need to be prepared to revaluate yourself, as you might find out things you never realised. Give yourself time to let the ideas sink in, before you try hunting down the person you 'just know' wrote it. This is not how we treat our auditors!

If you don't want to go through the Winner's Bible website, you can also set up a survey yourself through a website such as SurveyMonkey. Make sure you keep the responses anonymous (this will help other people feel more at ease about being truthful), and you need to try to get a decent number of people to respond. If only your mum responds, it's not anonymous, or very useful.

If creating your own survey, you need to ask questions to see how they perceive you, how they think you come across, and what they think are your strengths and weaknesses. Ask for specific examples so you can get a better idea of your unintentional cues.

I know it's scary, but it is important to understand how you really come across to people if you are trying to engineer your self-representation. So no skipping this step.

Once you have the results, compare with your own findings. How self-aware about your presentation are you?

Do you have as positives things other people put down as weaknesses? If you find out that others perceive you significantly differently to how you perceive yourself, then this is not a great sign.

For the purposes of creating an online profile:

     1. Try to work out what you are saying or doing which is giving the wrong impression.

     2. Make sure you get someone else to read your profile before you post it, because the chances are you won't see the unintentional signals you are giving off.

     For the purposes of life, you might want to think about this and possibly see a counsellor. It is going to affect many aspects of your life if you don't appropriately communicate and represent yourself to others, from your romantic attachments through to workplace relations. You might find that with some help, life could become a whole lot easier.

PART THREE

INTERNET MARKETING

CHAPTER FOUR

MARKET RESEARCH

Introduction

In the last section we looked at why psychologists think you have every chance and right to succeed through online dating. This should have given you a positive outlook and helped you realise some of the things that might have been holding you back in the past.

Now we are going to draw on a different discipline to work out exactly what we want to achieve from online dating – internet marketing. Obviously, any tools that can successfully sell a product online can help you sell yourself in the same medium. The aim of internet marketing is to get people aware and attracted to a product. Replace that with a human being, and that's pretty much what you want to do as well.

Oh, are you thinking that I'm objectifying you? Well, basically, yes I am. If you want to sell like hot cakes, you've got to be prepared to be compared to bits of heated dough with maple syrup. You need to realise that when it comes to choosing partners, people want to know a lot of the same of information as when buying a product: what are the benefits/features? How will it fit into my life? Why would I be interested in this model?

So, this part of the book is broken up into three sections which will help you make the most out of the principles of internet marketing. First we are going to look at market research. This is so often overlooked when starting to date online. However, if you don't know what's out there and what your ideal girl is looking for, how are you going to know what to write to be noticed? Also, with more people choosing to date online, there are more options available, which means more competition. We need to work out how we can make you stand out from the crowd, and who you want to stand out to!

Second, we are going to take this information and apply it to creating a brand – you – encapsulated in terms and with cues appropriate for your target market.

Then finally we are going to look at finding your appropriate avenue: choosing the best dating sites for you. Not all sites are created equal, and a little bit of research and thought will save you a whole lot of heartache and frustration later on down the road.

So, grab your self-reflective glasses, box full of hopes and dreams, a good dose of humour and follow me!

Why You Need To Do This

Have you ever started or thought about starting a business? The first piece of advice all business mentors give, and is embedded within the business plan, is to do your market research. Before you even begin to start developing a product or building the business, you need to research the market for a number of reasons. And they are good reasons. And they apply just as much to marketing yourself as a product on an internet dating site as they do to selling shoes. You can't sell anything where there's no market for it. You either need to change the product or find/develop the market.

Please don't be put off because I said you were a product. Of course you are a product, we all are. And you want to be bought. By a very specific customer, yes. And with no money changing hands because that is a totally different proposition. But in general, you want to go out into the wide world, find someone you have never met, present them with your features and benefits, hope that they decide you are worth taking a chance on, and then maybe even take you home and let you make them breakfast in the morning (well, let's not get ahead of ourselves). When it all boils down, there is a reason dating profiles used to be called 'personal advertisements'. That's what it's all about, making an attractive 'sell copy', making sure what you bring to the table is in a language that your ideal partner will understand and appreciate.

So, where do we need to start? We are going to assume that the overall product is viable, that if you are prepared to put in the effort to find a market, do correct advertising, packaging and promotion, then you will find at least one customer within your target range. And luckily for us, one good customer is all we need for this product. So, let's look at the other issues.

1. First we need to work out your target market. You don't want to be taken home by just anyone. The difficulty that faces us, but is quite uncommon in business, is that probably 80% of customers are not going to be appropriate for our product. So we need to work out what that 20% looks like.

2. Then begins stalker time – ahem, I mean 'market research' time. We need to make sure a) that your ideal woman actually exists online, and b) that she is looking for a product like you. What does your ideal customer want? This might involve realising that you are targeting the wrong market and that you need to go back and rethink your audience. This is okay, it is much better to work all that out now than have to go through months of no replies because you are contacting the wrong people.

3. Next we are going to do some keyword research. Assuming you have some of the characteristics you think your target market is looking for, how can you best represent that to them? This is part of making sure what you are communicating is the same as what they are interpreting. You might think you are suggesting you are active because you say you are 'sports-mad', but they

might interpret that as sitting in front of the TV all weekend watching footy. To be effective, you need to know their terminology.

4. Then we need to scope out the competition. How are they presenting themselves? Can you steal any ideas? Are there features you should be playing up to make you stand out? We'll scope out the best because if it works for them, there is no reason it can't work for you. Also, we'll see some of the worst, so you know what to avoid (and you will soon realise why I've written this book, and how many people need help writing their profiles).

Target Markets

There is an internet marketing saying: 'The riches are in the niches.'

What do they mean by this? If you try to create a product that is very general, yes you have more theoretical customers but a) you also have more competition and b) your customers are less invested because the product isn't specifically targeted to them.

So, if you think your ideal woman is 'blond and beautiful', that's a very broad category. Further, women who fit under that category will have very different preferences. Some of them might want men who are tall and strong, others might want men who earn lots of money, or who are healthy and active, who love computers, etc., etc.

However, if you narrow it down to women who are 'blond, have a college level education, live in Seattle, and love Mel Brooks movies' then it will be much easier to appeal to them and work out what they want.

If you manage to 'niche down' (focus on a smaller group within a large one) then you'll have less competition, appeal more and be found more easily.

So, it's time for some (more) brainstorming!

On another piece of scrap paper (need to think about the environment) or on your computer is fine as well (though it doesn't give you as much freedom to make wide, sweeping connections and diagrams, which I enjoy) I want you to brainstorm the different things you are looking for in your perfect match. Divide them up into 'must have', 'negotiable', and 'complete turn offs' just to help.

Think about:
- Physical attributes
- Personality traits
- Employment/income
- Situation (divorced/single mother etc.)
- Future goals
- Interests

Though you should list the things you want in a partner, even at this stage avoid making it appear like a simple laundry list. Add examples and reasons why you want these features, so you understand exactly what you are asking for. And keep in mind that no one person will satisfy all your wants. Be flexible.

Start with as many ideas as you can, then start defining them into a shorter and shorter lists. But keep in mind, we want to identify a market segment, not knock out all available options.

If you could choose only four things to define your partner, what would you look for? If you could choose just one interest, one physical attribute, one thing about their past and their current situation, what would it be? For example, I don't mind if a guy has blond hair or dark hair, but if I had to choose one physical attribute, I would prefer him to be taller than me. I don't mind at all what sort of music he likes, but he must love reading - anything and almost everything. How else am I going to get feedback on my novels?

Some tips on how to think about your ideal partner:

1. Don't list attributes that are necessary to any successful relationship such as 'honest' and 'trustworthy'. As very few people present themselves as 'dishonest' and 'untrustworthy' (and if they did, how would you know they were being honest about being dishonest? Maybe the dishonesty is in saying they are dishonest!). Therefore, you don't need to list these as it won't help define your market.

2. Try not to list negatives such as 'I don't want someone fat.' Always think of people in a positive light, and this will shine through in your writing. So, even when writing just for yourself, phrase it positively, such as 'I want someone active and slim', so there is no judgement on women who might be heavy.

3. Can you make your subjective statements more objective? For example, say you do want someone slim, what exactly does that mean to you? Can you be more specific? (I was totally surprised when watching a movie with my brother he said 'Oh, that actress is way too skinny!' I was like, 'What are you talking about, that's my ideal body shape.' Guys and girls generally have very different ideas of 'slim'.) A more reasonable way to frame it is: I would like someone within a healthy BMI range.

4. You need to list some fixed attributes (such as height) and then some of the things found in a person's general text (such as 'plays bass guitar'). This will help you search and strike up conversation. If you just have specific attributes in mind, it is difficult to know what to say when contacting them. A conversation based on 'Oh, I see you are five foot ten, tell me about that,' is pretty hard to maintain. On the other hand, if you only list interests, it is going to be very hard to search for her within the site as most of the sites have search categories based on fixed attributes such as age, not on general interests. So we want to cover both bases.

When you think you are done, draw up a table with four columns. We are going to be using this table for a while, so keep it handy. In the first column list all the important attributes you want your ideal woman to have.

Finished? Happy with the results? Good, let's move on.

Research

So, in the first column you have listed the top attributes you are looking for. Hopefully you have been honest and listed what really matters to you, and not sold yourself short in what would be a good match for you. As the psychology section demonstrated, most attributes are assessed relatively, so don't be afraid.

Based on the attributes listed, in the second column I want you to list what a woman who met your requirements might be looking for. Look back at the psychology section if you have to and start off by trying to take a guess at what she might want. This is an interesting exercise in how well you understand what particular women might be looking for and how they phrase it. So don't skip this step. Actually write it down so you can compare it later. Choose particular key words you think they might use. Would their ideal partner be 'creative' or 'artistic'?

Have you had a go?

Good, now we are going to see if your ideal woman exists, and exactly what she thinks she's looking for. It might sound calculated, but there is nothing wrong with doing a bit of research. We are looking for two things. First, does the list of attributes you want actually occur together? Have you become so specialised in your desires that it is unlikely you will ever find someone like that? Are you being unrealistic expecting her to be a size zero and love beer and burgers? The second thing we are looking for is 'keyword research'. Just as when you start a website, you would see which words are being most searched for in Google; now you want to see exactly how your target market is phrasing what they are looking for.

I recommend going to one of the big free websites, such as OK Cupid. You don't want to start creating your own profile just yet, because we haven't worked out how you are going to market yourself. So see if you can find a site that will allow you to search before you sign up.

The difficulty with most of these sites is that you have to search by objective attributes such as age, location, ethnicity etc. This won't help you find a sporty animal lover. However, you just have to live with this and spend a bit more time doing deeper research to find what you are looking for on each site. Specialised sites can help narrow the field, but many want you to sign up first, so not so useful at this stage.

So, see if you can find 10 profiles of women who roughly meet your description. Are they what you expected? Do you need to adjust some of your key terms for a better match? Or are you pretty happy with what you have found?

If you are happy, take the next step: look at what they say they want in a partner. It won't all be exactly the same, but are there some key attributes that are common to most of the profiles? Write them down in the third column of your table. Then compare to the column where you wrote what you thought they would be looking for.

The big question: were you totally wrong? Are there characteristics on all the profiles you chose that you underrated? Overrated? Ignored altogether? You can learn a lot from this information, so look for areas where you are likely to accidentally misrepresent yourself. Write down the words and concepts they use to describe what they are looking for, as we want to try and base your profile keywords on this (assuming this is true of you, of course).

Now, if you are still happy with the characteristics for women you have chosen, and don't find what these women want completely daunting, then you can move onto the next step.

Need a Plan B? In some cases you will find that all the women you can find that match your 'ideal' description are looking for something very different to you. So, what should you do? Take this as a reality check, and do some thinking. Is there something inherent within the attributes you desire which would suggest they wanted a particular type? For example, if it's absolutely essential to you that your ideal woman has a PhD, then they are most likely going to want someone at least with a university education. If you didn't finish high school, well then you have really only three options: change your 'essential' criteria for the woman of your dreams, go back to school, or try glossing over your credentials until they get to know you.

Option 1 is the fastest and most likely for success. While I don't want you to sell yourself short, you also need to be realistic. She needs to want you as much as you want her, and so aim for someone who is going to think you are a total catch. Option 2 is a long term view, and could turn out making you a better, higher achieving person. If there is something you really want, then you work for it. That's how the world works. Work out what your ideal woman would want, and try working to become it (before meeting them! Otherwise it's just sad. Before — good, after — sad.) Then there is option 3. It is the easiest option right now, but might cause a few awkward situations later on. You are welcome to try it, and there is always a chance that if you meet all her other criteria she will not care. However, in my experience, a deal breaker is a deal breaker, and when I specifically mention what I'm looking for and people contact me who ignore that, I get annoyed. Honestly, you're better off reevaluating why you want that particular attribute, and seeing if there is another way to get the end result you were interested in. Instead of saying she must have a PhD, do you actually mean that she has a good general knowledge and would be happy to talk philosophy over dinner?

Never be afraid to come up with a Plan B.

Your Competition

It's time to check out the competition. Why? Because you want to make sure that you come across as a unique proposition and avoid the big mistakes. What a lot of guys (and I would believe girls) don't realise is that their profile sounds exactly like a hundred others the user has read in the last hour. The same phrases, jokes, 'witty' comments, and self-deprecation make many otherwise great choices just seem bland and boring. You don't want that to be you.

So, go back to a big dating site and search under the same categories you will be listed in (according to your age, sex, race, religion, etc.). Have a read through and make sure that you can differentiate yourself. Also, keep a note of lines that keep coming up, and stay as far away from these as possible! The two from OkCupid questions that really bug me:

1. What are six things you can't live without? 'Air, Oxygen, Water, Food...' etc. Yeah, we get it, we all need those things to live. Does this tell me anything about you? No! And yet hundreds of guys use it.

2. What is the first thing people notice about you? 'Why don't you tell me?' So many guys use a variation on this that it's not funny (if it ever was). Just a warning.

Also, if someone has an absolutely brilliant profile, there is no harm in working out what makes it glow, and see if you can apply it yourself. Some sites will list the most popular matches in a category, the people who are being contacted/viewed the most. It's always worth checking out what these guys are doing. If they have a great photo, analyse how it was taken; the pose, lighting, props, etc., anything you can use as a model. Then read through their profile. What is their tone? Are they positive, funny, energetic, self-deprecating? The more you study the top guys, the more you will see how a good profile should be written.

While you are there, also look at some of the less successful profiles, if you can. People who haven't been contacted for a while, or whose photo and tagline make you want to cringe. As painful as it might be, make yourself read through their profile. Be objective and make a list of reasons why the profile doesn't work. Think of yourself as a consultant, and take the advice from this book and try to apply it to their writing. If you can see ways to improve their profile, it will help you improve your own. If nothing else, it will give you a big list of things not to do, which is always helpful.

So take your time. Just remember to clear your browser history and make sure that your views aren't coming up... could be hard to explain.

If you find a site that really doesn't have much competition in your field, then you need to ask yourself why. This could be a brilliant opportunity to find someone whose needs are not being catered for. Or, on the other hand, it could be because the site is not tailored to the types of partners you would be looking for. No competition is not always a good thing. However, if you can find at least a handful of girls who meet your requirements and could want something like you, it's probably worth a shot when we come to choosing sites.

Chapter Five

Creating A Brand

What Is Your Brand?

By now we have a lot of data about you, the market and your competition. It is time to put this altogether to come up with a brand or strategy.

As you might have noticed while doing your research, a lot of people start their profile by saying something along the lines of: 'I'm such a complex human being, I can't possibly be expected to express myself in just a few words.' First of all, it sounds arrogant because it suggests that everyone else who hasn't said this either isn't as complex, or hasn't realised it. Second, it suggests you have no self-awareness because you aren't able to summarise the important aspects of your personality. Third, it is also not actually that true. A good writer can express a multitude in just a few choice words. And add into that a couple of pictures (worth 1,000 words each) and you have more than this book!

Yes, you are very complex, but really so is a bottle of Coke. It could be marketed as a brilliant rust remover, a practical joke device when shaken, an all-nighter godsend, a family bonding experience, and so on. However, the Coca-cola company chose a very narrow set of concepts to encapsulate all that Coke is, because that is how branding works.

If you keep in mind that the aim of your profile is to spark the interest of your ideal partner, you'll realise that it is not about trying to express everything about you. Hopefully you will have a lifetime to work all that out. Instead, it is about packaging true parts of yourself in a way that are easily identifiable by your target market, appear honest and can be verified (think back to our psychology lessons). Therefore, everything in your profile needs to work together to support the brand that you are about to create.

So, let's look over the huge list of characteristics you wrote about yourself, including the information you gathered from friends and relatives. Now, I want you to cross reference that with what you discovered your ideal partner wants. Assuming that if you found you didn't match up, you went back to the drawing board about your ideal partner and came up with better fitting attributes to the women seeking you, you should now have a large number of matching attributes with no screaming contradictions.

Using your lists I want you to start by finding one of your characteristics that is a straight match to your ideal partner. People might not always list that they want someone with the same interest, but if you can find at least one shared one you will have more chance of having something to start the first conversation with and then connecting. Next, find two characteristics of yours that your ideal woman wants.

Have you found your three yet?

The next question is, do they present you as a reasonably well-rounded individual? You need to make sure that they don't cluster in an area, because it could make you sound a bit obsessed and lacking in any other interests. On the other hand, if there is no connection between them at all, it won't paint a very strong picture in someone's mind. As much as people hate being labelled, if it's going to happen, you want to be the one choosing the label. So, if you can get yourself branded as something like 'sporty but with a brain', or 'intelligent and arty' that is a lot better than 'the guy that likes this, does that a bit, and then has this other thing.'

Based on what you have come up with, add your attributes in the final column on your chart. It should have: your ideal woman, what you think she is looking for, what she is actually looking for, and what you bring to the table. By keeping in mind what she is looking for, you can make sure you are using appropriate terminology to describe yourself and your attributes. But remember, it might not be a perfect match – you are unique.

So, once you have three areas to focus on, you need to play with the wording of these so you find a balance between what is a true representation of your interest/attribute, the keywords your target market uses, and phrases that are emotive and paint a strong picture. Your aim is to come up with a one sentence summary that highlights the three chosen areas. Sadly I can't do that for you, so I'm trusting you to take a bit of time perfecting this. Go on, a little bit longer please. Perfect.

Once you have done that, it's time to write the evidence for your claims. If you can't back it up with evidence, then you aren't allowed to claim it. For example, if you said you were rich, intelligent and cultured, I want you to list on a piece of paper your net worth – assets, cashflow, passive income etc. – then your degrees or academic articles, and finally cultural events you have attended within the last six months. If these are not better than, say, 75% of the population, you can't really claim this as a unique selling proposition. Back to the drawing board and try again.

This exercise of providing evidence has two purposes. First, it will highlight if you are just kidding yourself about being able to claim certain words (don't feel bad, we all do it). Second, however, it will also show you if you have chosen concepts that are too vague. This is a mistake I see again, and again, and again. 'I'm fun-loving, down to earth and easy going.' Yeah, what exactly does that mean? If you can't give examples of times you have been 'fun-loving', or what you mean by 'down to earth', don't say it, it's just meaningless fluff.

Remember that you are creating yourself as a very niche product, so don't be afraid to bring in strange facts to support your brand, as this can help you stand out.

For the moment we are not including any of the negative qualities you worked out earlier. The branding is your advertising: you keep your product's major flaws out of the commercial.

So, completed all that?

Right, well now I want you to do it all again with a different set of words. It can be the same concepts, but expressed in different ways if you think you have nailed the perfect combination. Or you could choose completely different qualities.

Why do it again, you ask? Because you are an internet marketer, and every internet marketer will tell you that you need to do market testing. The best ideas usually aren't the first and you need alternatives to see which get a better response.

So finish the task, create two different branding options for yourself, so we can test which gets the best results.

Market Testing

For the best branding with the least embarrassment, we'll follow six steps of market testing. You could post everything online now but that runs the risk of your perfect girl coming across your profile while still in the testing stages. Therefore, I recommend going through these series of steps first to perfect your brand:

1. Read your branding out loud. Can you say it without cringing and going red? Your description should make you feel positive and like your best possible self. So keep working on it until it makes you feel good about yourself. (I remember the first time I called myself a writer to someone else. It made me feel so good, and more sure that writing was what I wanted to do.)

2. Pretend that you are sitting opposite an interested girl of your dreams. How would you describe yourself to her to convince her you're the best match? Does this match your branding? Yes, I want you to actually role play it with yourself. Say the conversation out loud because things always sound better in your head.

3. Next, do the grandma test. Would you be comfortable describing yourself this way to your grandmother? If not, why not? This should rule out being overly sexual or downright lying. Further, your grandmother may be old, but she is still a woman, and probably has gained a lot of insight into life over the years. So if you think she would laugh in your face, you might not have picked the best branding.

4. You need to find one other person, not related to you, to test your branding on. I don't really recommend calling in male friends for this part. The dynamics of male

friendship can often make it hard to be openly supportive of a soul-baring enterprise. You have gotten their advice on your attributes, and you will call on one or two of them again at the end to help you proofread and polish, so you don't need to bother them here. I recommend trying to find a female friend who is closest to your target market (but not the girl you have secretly had a crush on for years and years. If it hasn't happened, then let it go and give online dating a real chance. Don't use it to try to make her jealous.) Possibly the girlfriend or wife of a friend, who wants to help you but will understand there are no romantic undertones coming from you (and there aren't, right?). Approach them in such a way that will allow them to speak honestly. If you look like a sad puppy, they will find it harder to tell you that the branding sucks. And it is definitely better to find out now than later.

5. Now I want you to do the first date test: can you speak for at least ten minutes on each of these areas? If on the first date your ideal woman starts with 'Oh, you're a snowboarder, that sounds so interesting...', can you make sensible and interesting conversation? If not, tweak your branding so it suggests questions and conversation starters you feel comfortable with. (When I first started out, I made an off-handed comment in my profile about coffee, which sounded good but I don't actually drink all that much. Of course that was the first thing a cute guy picked up on and asked me how I liked it. I had to confess to my fib, which was not a good start. My bad.)

6. This last step has a slightly different purpose, but is just as important. Once you think you have your branding pretty much straight, then I want you to internet stalk yourself. That's right, type your name into Google, check out your Facebook and LinkedIn profiles, and see what comes up. If a girl gets your name, what will she find? Does it support your branding, or does it suggest you have made everything up? If you find a serious discrepancy, then there are two things you can do: one is to change your branding to be a bit more realistic. Or two, if you think your branding is a true representation of you and everything else is out of date or not rounded enough, go through and update your internet presence. You need to be able to support your branding online and off.

Your branding should now be good to start implementing. Hooray, and well done!

CHAPTER SIX

CHOOSING YOUR SITES

Find The Best Medium

Having worked out our market and branding, we now need to develop an advertising strategy. The advertising done by big companies can sometimes give us useful tips about how we can market ourselves, but they are not always the most useful. We might both be trying to sell a product, but big companies like Starbucks are trying to sell the product thousands of times by making it cheap and available to lots of people simultaneously. This is not what we are going for. For a closer parallel, think about a real estate agent selling your house. There is only one product, but they are trying to get the best possible price by finding multiple potential buyers. So, what do they do?

First of all, they don't advertise in just one place. A really good marketing campaign for a property will have the house listed online, in the company's window and catalogue, in the local newspaper, and possibly in a larger newspaper or specialised magazine as well. The same goes for you. If you want, you can just go to one of the largest sites and hope that is all you need to do, but you have a much better chance if you have your profile up on a number of different sites.

Second, successful real estate agents choose their advertising medium very carefully. You don't see houses across the state advertised in the local paper. But you do see certain price brackets being targeted towards different advertising avenues. Houses that are in a very high price bracket might be advertised in some of the architectural magazines, but they wouldn't do the same with a three bedroom, two bathroom brick veneer house. Why not? Because while the people reading the magazine are interested in general in buying houses, it's a different kind of house they're looking for. You need to know where your target market will be looking.

So, after spending so much time working out your target audience for your dating profile, it would be silly now to ignore all that and just upload your profile to any old site. Therefore, you need to do some research into which is the best site for you to list on, remembering you want to be in more than one place and targeted to your audience for the best possible results.

Types of Sites

If you hadn't realised, there are literally millions of online dating sites catering for almost every niche market. However, they break down into three basic types. First are the general dating sites where you upload your profile, can search other people's and anyone can contact anyone else. These sites can be either free or charge a fee (up front or to contact someone). The advantages of this type of site is that you are free to browse and don't have to rely on the site's 'formula' for what makes a perfect match.

Some disadvantages include not being targeted enough to the audience you want to attract, and being contacted frequently by people who are not at all like what you said you were interested in. For example, even though I live in Australia and say I want someone very close to me, I am constantly contacted by men who live in different countries! I've had men from Kuwait, Indonesia, many parts of Africa, Malaysia, and a lot of other non-English speaking countries contact me. I do wonder whether they are hoping I will help them move to Australia. Not going to happen, just saying now.

Second are the matchmaking sites where you give them your details and what you are looking for, and they suggest partners for you. These sites are generally paid services. The advantages include the fact that once people have to pay, they are generally more serious. Also, the matchmaking system can stop people who are totally unsuitable from contacting you. However, the disadvantages are that on some of the sites, you can't contact someone unless the site recognises you as a match. This is difficult because the algorithms that some of the sites use don't actually have any basis as to making a good match. eHarmony, one of the giants in the field, was studied by a group of psychological researchers led by Finkel who concluded that 'no compelling evidence supports matching sites' claims that mathematical algorithms work.'

The third type are the speciality sites that focus on niche areas. There are very large areas such as Christian dating sites, or more specific sites such as Trekkie in Utah dating sites. These services can be free or paid. The advantages are that you can focus on your niche area and know that at least one of your interests or attributes is generally guaranteed. Though, I will put in a note that having tried a number of Christian dating sites, it becomes very apparent that while dating a Christian is a requirement for me, it is not the only requirement! There are many people who are just as unsuitable for me, despite being Christian. While using a niche site helps you make sure at least one attribute is a definite match, people often write their profiles focusing on that attribute and might not tell you anything else. On Christian sites there are a large number of profiles which appear to only talk about God and suggest that the user has no other interests but loving God. I'm all for loving God, but I also want to know that the guy does some other things in his life as well.

Paid or Free?

Free sites may appear initially very attractive. I chose OkCupid because it was free and large. However, there are a lot of problems with free sites. First of all is the increased creep factor. I don't know if this translates across the same to men looking for decent women, but as a female I have been contacted with a lot of very strange offers by men that I doubt would bother to sign up to a paid site. Also, there are a growing number of profiles on free sites that are actually hidden advertising for paid services for other businesses. I can't be sure, but I did get contacted by one 'person' who had a profile purely set towards offering threesomes, providing either men or women. I suspect if I had been interested in this, it would have come at a cost. As it was, they were very rude when I was not interested.

Another problem with the free sites is that some use your details for advertising. I understand that a lot of sites can use your photo as advertising for the site, but some actually use your email and details to create marketing lists. This is something you would need to think about if you wanted to protect your privacy (this is one of the reasons we'll be researching our sites before signing up).

Many sites have a free introductory period or level, and then for additional features or to stay on the site you need to pay. You need to be careful and do you research into these sites, because there are reports of problems signing up for the 'free' introductory period. Particularly, if the site asks for your credit card details up front. There have been cases where sites have started charging the credit card after the trial period, regardless of whether the person actually continued to use the site. There have been complaints that even when the profile has been cancelled within the trial period, the credit card has still been charged later.

Paid sites generally range between $10-$60 per month. There are of course some very expensive sites in specialised niche areas, but this in itself is a filtering tool. If you aren't able to pay, you are probably not appropriate for the niche market. The difficulty with paid sites is that often you aren't allowed to see if there are any suitable candidates until you actually sign up, so it could be a complete waste if it turns out they don't have any profiles close to your target market. Also, it has been found that some of the owners of paid sites 'create' profiles themselves to attract more people to sign up.

So, these are things you need to be aware of before signing up. Overall, if you are serious about finding a partner, and have made it a priority in your life, you should probably have at least one paid profile. Think of it as an investment in your future.

Managing Your Strategy

Choosing appropriate sites is all about having a strategy. You know what your goal is, so you need to develop the best advertising strategy to achieve it. Start by doing some in depth research. Look at the dating site options available in your area and in any niche markets you want to target. Make a list of paid and free sites, with a variety of general, matchmaking and specific sites. Try to get about 20 possible sites, covering all options.

Decide how many you are going to sign up to at one time. Keep in mind that you will need to visit all of them frequently to keep your profile active. This will keep you at the top of a lot of lists, and make sure you turn up when people search 'online within the last n number of days'. Also work out what your budget is and how many paid sites you want to manage at one time. Finally, keep in mind that you will want to change sites every few months (assuming you haven't found your perfect match by then). Changing sites is a great tactic, because it is always good to be the new guy in town. I took down my profile for a couple of months while I was doing other things. But when I came back, I saw a lot of faces I had seen months ago. This did not come across as a good sign or make them more attractive.

Got your list of sites? Good. Now that you know how many sites you are about to target, it's time to do background checking into those sites. You do not want to put your personal details up on just any site. After all this effort, for the sake of your safety and future happiness, it is worth spending at least 10 minutes for each site Googling reviews. What do people say about the site? Have they been in the news for misconduct? Do people recommend it or are all the reviews about bad experiences? Some people will always post negatively, but if you find any serious red flags, or can't find any positive reviews (except for what the site puts out itself), then it's better to walk away and try somewhere else before you are committed.

In Conclusion

Choosing your site is an important part of your overall online dating success. It doesn't matter how great your profile is, or how much research you've done into your perfect match. If you load this up to a site with no one matching your ideal, you aren't going to get anywhere. Further, doing some simple research now can drastically cut the potential danger of online dating. So, remember:

1. You want to try a few different sites at the same time, to give yourself the best exposure.

2. Try a mix of general dating, matchmaking and niche sites. The disadvantages should even themselves out, as long as you are prepared to say 'no' to a lot of people.

3. Always do research before signing up to any site. What are people on the internet saying about it? Does it have good reviews or are there serious concerns being raised about it?

4. If you can, always try to check that they have a suitable number of profiles in your target market before you sign up. If it is a paid site and meets all your other criteria (you've researched it, it isn't too expensive, it

covers your target market), then sign-up to the free introduction first; just be prepared to take action if it's not what you want in the end.

5. Be prepared to pay for these services, because it is worth investing in your happiness.

6. Review your strategy from time to time, and be prepared to change sites every few months if it is not working.

We come to the end of the internet marketing section. By now you should have all the strategies and tricks to understand how to target your market and what branding you want to present. These are the steps that a lot of people skip, but I'm sure you realise now how vital they are for success. You might hit it lucky without them, a lot of people do, but why wouldn't you want to be more in control of the outcome of this adventure?

However, as much as I love the psychology and the tactical side, now we come to my favourite part of it all: the storytelling.

PART FOUR

CREATING THE STORY

CHAPTER SEVEN

THE IMPORTANCE OF STORIES

Introduction

The world is made up of stories. Please don't think this is a bad thing, that it is all propaganda and manipulation. Stories are the essence of humanity; they help us make sense of the world, and they also make it a more interesting place to live. We don't want life to be just about getting up and going to work every day. We need to believe that there is more, that this is an echo of a quest humans have been on for centuries, and that someday we will get the chance to be the hero of our own story. Stories are an ingrained part of our psyche, and help us in a number of ways. We are going to use them to make your profile more effective and memorable.

One of the best mnemonic tools for remembering a list of abstract words is to create a story. You can pick any list of words, and if you just try to learn them by rote you won't be nearly as successful as if you can connect them into a story. Here are some random words I've grabbed by flicking through a book: number, months, brothers, story, replaced, phantom, shot, prepare, nature, work, remember. If you tried to remember each word individually, you would have no aid to get from one word to the next. Our brains like connections, they like things to make sense. This is where stories come in. Stories make connections between abstract concepts. So a great way of remembering this list of words is to think 'a number of months later the brothers were sitting around telling a story about how one of them had been replaced by a phantom. They had been shot, so the phantom had prepared a special medicine from nature, and it worked! They remembered this for the rest of their lives.

Silly, yes. More effective? Much.

Tricks Of The Trade

So why am I telling you this? Well, you want to stand out and be remembered, don't you? Then you need to tell a good story. Your brand is all about presenting what would otherwise be a random collection of attributes, experiences and interests as an integrated story. This will make your profile appeal to your reader; they can experience a deeper connection to you because you make more sense to them, and it helps them to remember you even after they have gone offline. These are all highly desirable outcomes.

So, I am going to let you in on some of the secrets of creating a great story. These are the tools of the trade for writers.

1. *Show, don't tell.* Any writer will have heard this a hundred times. It means you shouldn't force information onto the reader, you should let them experience it and draw their own conclusions. For example, you want them to think you are intelligent. Writing in your profile 'I am intelligent' is not nearly as effective as 'my university paper on the themes of women's liberation in Jane Eyre was published in a leading academic journal'.

2. *Structure.* Every story has a structure. It has a beginning, middle and an end. The structure reinforces the purpose of the story. There are a couple of different types of structures, and they have different purposes, but good, memorable stories are not just randomly chucked down on a piece of paper. We expect there to be order. Despite the dissected nature of the online profile – height over here, movies over there, photo in the top right hand corner – there still needs to be structure within it all. It should have an introduction, main body and conclusion. The intro is a nice summary of your main points, the body goes through each point and gives examples, and the conclusion reinforces the points and leaves the reader with something to think about.

3. *Focus.* Remove extraneous pieces of information from the story. We don't find out that Little Red Riding

Hood also visited the baker on Tuesdays, unless this would be important knowledge to the story. While writing your profile, it might feel like there are many different parts to be covered, however you should use your branding to make sure you focus on the important parts. If you like your three key attributes into a story, this can help you stay focused. Think of it just like a Coke ad. *If my life were like a Coke ad, it would start with my elaborate and clever plan to get your attention (intelligent), there would be a scene where you were impressed as I stripped off my Coke drenched T-shirt (good-looking), and finish with us laughing on the beach (sense of humour).* If you think your clever, hot and funny, why not?

4. *The hook.* You need a hook to grab them at the beginning. The first line of a book is always the most important, and hardest to write. It needs to introduce the flavour of the book, as well as sucking the audience in. If the first line isn't interesting, most people won't keep reading. The same goes for your profile, which we will discuss more under Creating Your Tagline.

5. *Find your voice. How* you say something is just as important as *what* you say. Your word choice indicates a lot about you, and taking time to find the right word can make the difference between a boring or fascinating story. You want to make sure that your writing style reflects your branding. For example, using a lot of slang might undercut your assertion that you are educated and cultured. But similarly, using a lot of highbrow words will conflict with your image of being a down-to-earth, nice guy. (Which, by

the way, is not a branding you should have gone for, as it is meaningless. Hopefully you picked that up when trying to come up with evidence for it.)

6. *Pacing.* How you write, the punctuation and words you use can have a physical effect on your reader. If you increase the pace of your writing, the reader will start breathing faster, getting more excited (or anxious, depending on the nature of the story) and have more adrenaline pumping through their body. If you slow the pacing you can soothe them, help them relax, and occasionally send them to sleep. Therefore, you want to pick the pacing for your free writing section that mirrors your branding. If you are aiming for cultured and refined, a slower pace would be more appropriate. If you are going for adventurous and sporty, then you want a faster pace. So, how do you get these different paces? Two simple tricks you can use are punctuation and word choice. More full stops and shorter words with sharp consonants will give a faster pace. Or, more commas and longer words with long vowels will give a slower pace. It's pretty simple once it's pointed out, and you might have been doing it subconsciously in places. However, now you can make your writing more consistent and fix it if you need to. (Of course, don't get carried away and make nonsense sentences. It still needs to read well.)

So, keeping those basics in mind, let's get onto writing your actual profile!

CHAPTER EIGHT

CHOOSING A NAME

The Starting Point

Yes, finally, after all those hours of research and practice, we are finally here. You are writing your profile. The very first thing that you will need to decide on is your name (or handle).

Now, if you browsed through the table of contents, thought everything else looked boring, and have jumped straight to the action – shame on you. As they say, 'if you fail to plan, you plan to fail.' Go back now and at least attempt most of the work before this point. Otherwise, I completely wash my hands of you and your success, though recommend you keep reading as it will be better than doing nothing at all. Hopefully you will come to see the error of your ways.

Everyone who has done their homework, you have my permission to feel smug. You have set yourself up for success.

Right, now, back to the name. Other than your profile picture, your name is the next major influencer of whether a girl will click on your profile or not. Keep in mind that when you send a message, she will usually receive an email first saying 'TomCat has just sent you a message.' Whether she opens that email or clicks through depends a lot on how attractive or off-putting your name is. So, tread wearily, my young padawan.

With your branding fresh in your mind, hopefully you will have a few ideas for what an appropriate name might be. Now write down a few more, just in case, because the biggest problem is that whatever name you have in mind, it is most likely already taken. I know that at OkCupid they make great suggestions like adding 'taco' or 'megatron' to the end of it. Seems funny, but I really don't suggest you do it. Whatever effort you have put into creating a brand can be undermined in a single move (unless your brand was 'Mexican food lover', in which case, go for it).

So clearly you want a name that reflects your branding. And yet, there are so many different ways to do that. As I don't know your particular branding, I can't make recommendations. However, I can take you through the pitfalls others have fallen into, as examples of what not to do.

What Not To Do

Let me walk you through the maze that is your name. Firstly, things to avoid. You are, of course, welcome to disagree on any point, I'm just telling you turns me off. However, there is usually some common sense in my advice, which you might see once it has been pointed out. Please note that this advice is aimed towards most dating sites, and might not apply to very select specialty sites such as S&MRUS.

1. The Offensive Name

On the one hand, I would like to believe that I would not need to list this one out. On the other hand, the evidence suggests that I do. Blanket statement – any name that makes a girl feel dirtier for having read it should not be used on most dating sites.

Obviously it also disqualifies you from the 'nice guy' category, so you shouldn't be reading this book. However, if you have picked up this book, and have gotten this far in hopes of learning something, and yet think this might be an appropriate form of introduction, I really don't think I can help you. On a general dating site, I don't expect to be dragged into the gutter when searching for potential partners. Save the smut for specialised sites.

This includes anything with swear words in it (really, that is your brand?), or focuses primarily on sexual acts (just pay your money and get a hooker). Any sort of fetish or personal sexual preference shouldn't be the first thing you share about yourself either. You are a person first.

2. Misspelt Words

So we all acknowledge that there are limited names, and if you just change the spelling you can get the same effect... generally. However, you need to make sure it doesn't come across as an inability to use the English language properly. Having said that, this applies more if your target market is a native and educated English speaker. If, on the other hand, you are focused on non-native speakers, or are not fussed about education, this probably does not matter nearly as much. This is the advantage of having done your research first.

3. Names That Are Questions

This one might not be as obvious, but I recommend caution when considering a name that is a question, such as 'RUthe1' (I made that up, so sorry to anyone who has used it!). There is the advantage that in asking a question, the reader's mind automatically tries to answer it, so you have gained more of their attention. However, the disadvantage is that when searching internet sites, people are defensive and looking for faults. Human nature is perverse. If you state something like that, more often than not the mind will automatically think the opposite, 'No', and move on without looking further.

Also, questions like 'are you the one?' make you come across as insecure and needy. Yes, it is a dating site, but you don't want to come on too strong. If, within seconds of introduction, you force someone to contemplate whether there is any long term future between you, you will scare away a lot of girls.

4. A Subjective Opinion As A Statement

This is more difficult, because in one way your branding is a subjective opinion of yourself (which you are going to support with as much evidence as possible, aren't you?). However, keep in mind that if you say 'I'm super sexy' before I've gotten to know you, all I'm going to think is 'Nah, not really.' Any name that might make someone want to cut you down to size, I'd stay away from. (Though that might be a particularly Australian trait...). Just remember, it's up to me to decide if you're sexy.

5. Having a Random Number on the End

We all know there is a limit to the number of names out there, so taking JohnSmith8 would appear to be an easy solution. However, I would be cautious about this, because it makes you look like a follower and not very original. It is much better to try to be the first. And if you can't manage that, a better option I saw was putting the number on the front and back, so 8JohnSmith8. Your potential dates are less likely to read that as you're the 8th John Smith, and instead just focus on the name in the middle.

6. Acb321fx60

Finally, it is quite surprising the number of people who have a random collection of letters and numbers as their name. Sure, there's much less competition for that name. But there's a good reason for that! And it's a total failure in branding. You have wasted your first impression opportunity.

Also, if things start to take off, and the girl has to talk about you to her friends, what is she going to call you? Her friends will probably make up some embarrassing code name, and then she will have to call it off with you because every time she goes to say your name, all she is thinking is 'dognoodle' (maybe she has weird friends, what can I say?).

Three Good Ideas

There are plenty of things to avoid when choosing a name. But what should you be looking for?

You want three basic things in a name:

1. A good first impression – start plugging your branding.

2. Something easy to remember and say.

3. Security – don't give away actual personal details as you don't know who's stalking you.

With that said, I'm going to leave you to work out possible names. Remember that on more niche sites there won't be as many people competing for names, so you might be able to get your first preference. However, on the larger sites, be prepared with backups.

CHAPTER NINE

PICTURE THIS

What's In A Picture?

Your picture is worth 1000 words, and 100 dates.

Raise your hand if you hoped you might be able to do all this without putting up a picture?

Now also put up your hand if you hoped you could use a selfie from your phone or an old photo with other people in it?

Have I Taught You Nothing?

Yes, you do need a photo. That is non-negotiable if you are serious about this. Nope, not negotiating. And yes, you will probably need to take a few photos just for your profile. But no, they cannot be selfies.

You have spent hours and days researching your market and creating your brand. Why would you then miss out on opportunities to show off all that work?

As mentioned in the psychology section, online dating is very limited in the cues that are given, so people read more meaning into the ones that remain. In order to come across as honest, you need to support what you are saying with as much evidence as possible. Your photo is one of the strongest supports you can give, because it is the least manipulable. (Yes, you can Photoshop it, but that is way harder than just typing 'I'm super sexy'. Think about it.) So you need a photo – well, actually a few.

Not only do you need them, but you need them to look good. Thinking of putting up a shot you've clearly taken yourself? This immediately says that you have no friends, because you couldn't find one single other people who could hold the camera for you.

To help you out, I'm going to go through the most common mistakes I've found online, and what these photos are actually screaming. Then, I'm going to send you out on a photo shoot! Yah!

The Bad

Remember that the profile picture is not just being used to judge your appearance, but your entire life. So, here are some things to be aware of:

1. Having a Picture of Something Else
There are a number of people out there who include a picture of a sunset or a dog as their primary photograph. I can't decide if this is better or worse than

not having a photo at all. It might support your branding a bit better than nothing, but overall it does not come across well. Why don't you want people to see your face? There could be a number of reasons, but none of them are good. Yes, you might want to show that you are a dog-lover, but this message is much more effective if you are also in the picture. Otherwise people think the message is that your dog is your more attractive side.

2. A Picture With Multiple People In It

Why would you do this? It seems ridiculous to me, but I've seen it so many times it's made the list. First of all, it shows that you haven't put any effort into creating your profile. You couldn't even be bothered to find a photo of just you. Second, every girl will always assume that you are the most unattractive guy in the photo. Now, if part of your branding is that you have really great mates, then you might want a photo of all of you doing things. However, this would not be your primary photo. And even then, there is always the risk of the girl going 'hmm... that other guy's pretty cute...'. So overall I don't recommend it. If you have to, recreate the photo with just you.

3. You with Another Girl

I assume the logic is that you are trying to prove you can pull hot girls. This is slightly undermined by the fact that you are on an internet dating site. Further, users will judge the girl in the photo (harshly, it's human nature) and then assume that is your type. Even if the girl in the photo is an exact representation of your target market, after she has gone through this filter you will find no other girl wanting to own up to being like her. Therefore, every girl viewing it will assume you are looking for someone else.

The only acceptable woman ever would be your grandmother. Your mother makes you look like a mama's boy. Having a child in your photo is okay if it is yours and you want to get across clearly that you have children and are a loving parent. If you want to get across that you are great with children, but don't have any of your own, then put a niece or nephew in one of your other photos, not your primary one, and clearly state it's not yours.

4. Comic Ugly Shot

Please keep in mind that it will be assumed that your worst shot is what you actually look like most of the time. It also seems that you are hiding behind humour because you are insecure about your looks. This is a killer for online attraction ratings. Confidence is what you are going for. Funny and still amazingly attractive is the branding you want.

5. The Decapitated Shot

At no point in your profile photos, even if you upload 100 of them, should you have a shot of your body without your head. It is disturbing, to begin with. Even if you have a great body and it is part of your branding to show it off, you can still zoom out that extra little bit to put your head in there. If you can objectify your own body, it suggests you are even worse at objectifying other people. It also completely undermines any suggestion that you are looking for a serious relationship.

6. This Is Me... 10 Years Ago

All of your photos need to be reasonably up to date, with the primary photo being taken in the last few months. You look great as you are, and have matured well, so be confident. It is usually pretty obvious if someone hasn't put up a recent photo, because no 40 year old actually looks like that. But even if you don't get found out now, you are just leading to in person rejection – not because you're bad looking, but because you are not what they expected. Now you look older and like a liar, or just seriously insecure, which is not attractive either. Even though a lot of people do feel that an out-dated photo is still legitimate, if you are prepared to put some time in now, you can definitely take an even better photo. Recreate your favourite shot if that makes you feel better, but add in some extra clues to your achievements since then.

7. This Is My Glamour Shot

While I am advising you to get some photos taken just for the purpose of your dating profile, I don't recommend using professional glamour photos. First of all, these are notorious for not looking like reality. Second, it comes across as a bit egotistical, that you pay to have photos taken of yourself for no reason (silly, as it's an awful lot of fun and a great way to spend a day, having done it myself). Instead, you want natural appearing photos. (Though, I admit that this is more of a problem for girls than it is for boys.)

8. The Drunken Shot

No. Not even if your branding is 'likes a good time'. You are not attractive when you are drunk. No one is. That's pretty much all I've got to say on this.

9. Out of Focus Shots

I'm going to include in this shots where you are not the focus, and landscape photos where you are just a speck. You do want the photograph to support your other attributes, which might include being outdoorsy. However, the main purpose of the photo is always showing that the other good looking photo wasn't a fluke. People want to see you. Clearly.

That is my big list of don'ts. Now, onto what actually makes a good photo.

The Good

So, now we come to staging your photo shoot. Hopefully you really do have a friend who is available to help you for a few hours without laughing too hard. Bribe them with dinner if you have to. If you can, beg, borrow or steal a reasonably good camera. You can use your iPhone if desperate, but better quality is worth the bother.

Before you start the photo shoot, it is time to do a little bit more research. I would recommend taking a few minutes to look at some magazine ads and spreads that include male models or actors. Go down to your local library if you have to and grab some women's magazines. They know what we like. If they can be in a particular niche area (Women's Fitness, for example) that is helpful too. (I'm often surprised at how differently males and females are portrayed in male versus female targeted magazines. Please don't base what you think looks good on male body building magazines!)

Start with advertising, because the whole point of an advertising shot is to create a story for you to buy into. The male model is not just selling you perfume, he is selling exciting holidays in the Caribbean, or sultry nights in Paris. Your branding should be as compelling and integrated as the evocative images created by advertising campaigns. They know how to do it, so copy from the best.

When you have a few good examples, analyse them. Start with the pose. Look at the angle of their head, their eye contact, stances they take, and what they do with their hands (hands are tricky). Especially focus on any that tell a story you're interested in recreating. Note other elements you can emulate. What are they wearing? What background do they have? What props are they using? Look for photos with just one person in the shot, and see what you can do. Of course, be careful copying exactly a very famous picture, unless you are purposefully doing it to get a laugh. And then be aware of unfavourable comparisons (so he thinks he's as good looking as Brad Pitt, huh?).

Also, keep in mind the different types of photos that you will need.

Your photos can be divided into your main profile picture, which is really the most important and needs to make your target audience want to click on your profile, and your backup photos. These will be inside your profile, and also need to be just as good looking and well prepared, but can have more things happening in them to support your story.

The actual staging of each photograph will depend a lot on your target audience and the message you want to get across. Your photo doesn't need to appeal to everyone, just to those in your niche. However, here are some general points that have been found to be true.

1. Have some action shots in there, as it shows that you have a life someone else might be interested in being part of.

2. If you are not going to smile, make sure you have a really good reason for it. A smile makes you come across as confident, which is always a good thing.

3. Photos that are 'summery' are seen as more attractive than colder, winter photos. Try to recreate this with good lighting even if you are taking them in winter.

4. Have at least one photo that supports each different part of your branding. Looking just at your

photos should give people an overview of your whole message.

5. Include as your last photograph something that can start a conversation, something interesting and appeals to your target audience.

6. As much as I hate to admit, one picture of you with a cute animal is always a winner. Unless it is against your branding. Or dead. Or stolen.

7. Make sure you have included at least one close up. You want to eliminate the fear that you really have warts on your nose.

8. Then one full-length shot. We want to know what you look like from head to toe.

9. Finally, I don't know if I agree with this, but I'll put it in for you to decide. OkCupid found that the best pose for guys' pictures involve not smiling and not making eye contact. The second best is to smile but not make eye contact. Try experimenting with it and see if you can make it work for you.

When you have some ideas, discuss with your friend how you could create them. It is much easier trying to take a good photograph if you know what you want it to look like at the end. Just standing in front of a camera trying to be 'natural' is much harder than the models make it appear. So, do some research, a bit of practice in front of the mirror to get your expressions right, then go out and have some fun. If you need to, make a day of it and visit a series of different locations. Is there a local beach, cafe, climbing centre? Just make sure you change your wardrobe in between.

Don't be shy, have fun with it all.

CHAPTER TEN

GETTING PERSONAL

The Checklist

The next part of the profile is usually the personal details, which is just a checklist of different objective attributes such as height, eye colour, occupation, etc. It might not seem that important to fill this in, as a lot of the information might already be in your profile. However, keep in mind that this is the information which the sites usually use for their searches. So if you want your target market to be able to narrow down and find you, then you need to fill in as much of this information as possible.

The only part I would be cautious about is listing your income. While not stating your income could suggest it is low, it also implies that you don't want someone who is only interested in your money. If you have no problems with being judged on how much you earn, then I would put it in. But it is one of the few things I think is acceptable not to list.

The only other thing I have to say is not to lie, especially about things that will be found out eventually. Don't add inches to your height. If you have done your target marketing right, you will be aiming for women shorter than you. So what if another eight girls don't click because they are taller than you? They aren't your market. I also once had a guy lie about his ethnicity. It's hard to maintain that you're 'white' when your photos show otherwise (or else his photos were lying...) but either way it made him look like an idiot, and made me move onto someone else.

CHAPTER ELEVEN

SELF-SUMMARY FREESTYLE

The Free-Text Section

Now we get into the good bit, writing wise. Most online dating sites allow you to put in some free-text about yourself. On a side note: speed-dating sites usually don't have this, so if you are scared of writing, why not start off on one of these until you gain some more confidence?

Most websites will break the free section up into a series of boxes with a prompt such as 'What are you interested in?', 'What are six things you couldn't live without?' These are designed to help you turn a boring description into possible stories and mental pictures for your audience. As these vary from site to site, you shouldn't just copy and paste the same text into all the sites you sign up for. Of course, you wouldn't be doing that anyway, because you know that on each site you need to target your message particularly to that niche area. However, just in case you didn't think it through: yes, you will need to take the same basic concepts but write them out fresh for each site. Answering the questions appropriately and with a mind to the audience will make you appear more engaged and intelligent. If your answers are generic or off-topic, it will look like you don't have great comprehension skills and/or are boring. Not a good start.

We are going to look at the tagline first, and then general points about the self-summary. While not all sites will ask you to put in a separate tagline, you can still use it as the first sentence in a standalone paragraph if you need to. This will give your reader a quick snippet to entice them, before you seduce them with your great writing.

So, let's get straight into it.

The Tagline

You want to summarise your branding in one sentence. Other strategies such as using famous quotes or truisms are popular, which is why you shouldn't use them because 100 other guys already have. Unless there is a quote that totally encapsulates your branding, don't use it. It's a waste of a chance to express yourself, and ends up making you just another tired profile.

Luckily, you should have your killer beginning sentence already worked out from those exercises you did picking your three top attributes. You don't have to list all three, you could pick your main one and make it a one line story: 'When surfing in Hawaii I got bitten by a shark. But don't worry, none of the important parts are missing.'

Think of it like the first line in a book. It needs to give a sense of the type of book it will be, build atmosphere and make you keep reading. This is why writers agonise over their first lines, long after they have finished the rest of the book.

When writing it, think about the type of language you use. Your choice of language will be an immediate indication of your target market (whether you realise it or not). Do you use slang that only certain people understand? Does your use of abbreviations suggest a particular age group? Make sure your language portrays you exactly as you want it to, and that your target audience will understand it and be attracted by it. Particularly, be careful it is not male orientated. Just because your friends find it funny doesn't mean it is going to be a winner.

Also, you want to choose specific words that will build a quick but vivid image in the reader's mind. This picture needs to match the rest of your profile, and is a great opportunity to get your reader thinking along the lines you want them to continue on. To build a mental image quickly, the easiest way is to draw on preconceived ideas. Look for words with strong connotations. In the example above, Hawaii invokes images of sun and relaxed fun. It would have been a completely different image if I had said I was diving in Antarctica when I was bitten by a shark.

If you are struggling with the creative aspect of this, you can use your market research to help you target your tagline. What were the taglines used by some of your favourite female profiles? Can you turn that around (without looking creepy so it reads 'Yes Clarice, I have been reading your profile…')? Can you borrow and adapt from your competition?

Once you think you have something good, read it aloud. Do you stumble, does it sound awkward? If so, then keep crafting. If you can only get one thing to sound good, it should be this line.

When you think you've gotten the line down pat, and can say it like Humphrey Bogart in *Casablanca*, it's time to move on to the rest of your summary.

Structure

The structure of most free texts should follow a simple essay format: introduction, main body, conclusion. Your tagline is usually a standalone and is really more of a teaser than an introduction. So you will want just a few, maybe three, sentences to form an introductory paragraph. Here you will expound your three basic virtues that make up your branding as a quick summary of you for the reader to take or leave.

The main body can be spread across a couple of sections. If there are individual questions, you want to treat each one as a paragraph of the main body, relating to your introduction while expanding each point. A trap I've seen a lot of people fall into (and might have tripped into myself early on) is that they write everything they want to in the first section, then dutifully follow the structure and write it out again in the second part. And so on. This repetition results in a normal guy sounding obsessed with sports. Also, it is a boring read.

If you have a different point for each question, each bit will be a new revelation and therefore interesting, building a fuller picture of you. So please read through all the questions first and formulate your summary to incorporate all of them.

As with pictures, I'm going to guide you first by discussing what should be avoided. Then we'll look at ways to handle this section.

What To Avoid

A lot of my advice on what to avoid is just a mixture of good psychology, marketing and writing.

1. Any Negative Emotion

What do you think of when you imagine your ideal first date? Laughter, romance, excitement, maybe some nerves, and possibly some adrenaline pumping around? No one imagines a great first date conversation including whinging, scathing indictment of members of the opposite sex, snivelling, emotional manipulation or ambivalence. This would be a 'horror date'. So why do some people put it in their profiles? You need to think of your profile as a pick up line! Cheeky, funny, endearing. No one is endeared by 'Why doesn't anyone want to date me?' The only answer is: because you're a whiner.

2. Fence Sitting

Related to the point above, please reconsider saying that 'You're just checking this out' or 'A friend made me sign up'. It is a self-protection move, but it suggests you think anyone who is actually trying at this must be a loser. That is not attractive. No one wants to go on a date with someone who's not really sure if they want to be there. Try making the reader feel like they are the centre of your attention while they are there, that you find them fascinating and want to know more about them (but without being a stalker). Everyone loves feeling special, so do your best to compliment your reader. If you write your profile with the attitude that everyone who is going to read it will be a honest and interesting human, this will show through.

3. Statements In The Negative

This is a phrasing issue. Though it can be difficult, try to avoid making statements in the negative, 'I don't like...' etc. First of all, this comes across as picky, while on the other hand 'I love...' comes across as active and energetic. Further, negative clauses bring the very thing you are trying to avoid to the forefront of your reader's mind. Don't believe me? Don't think about elephants.

4. I'm Just Like 400 Hundred Other Men

As previously mentioned, don't used tired sentences that have no meaning. The majority of the world is 'fun-loving'. You want to be more specific and engaging than that. Being 'fun-loving' tells me nothing about you, except maybe that you fear there are people all around who don't love fun. This is why you worked out your brand with specific examples to paint real pictures for your audience. This will also help you target your niche. While 'fun-loving' might appeal to everyone, you will get closer to your perfect partner if you can find the other person who thinks it's fun to go to the beach in Victorian bathing suits before playing a game of croquet.

5. Giving Your Life Story

Hopefully you have worked this one out by my repeated (ad nauseam?) instructions about picking your key qualities and focusing just on those. However, in case you are inching towards the epic saga, draw back! Leave some mystery in the relationship, please, they haven't even met you yet. General rule of thumb: anything you wouldn't say on a first date shouldn't be in your profile. Save it for date two, or five, or after the wedding.

6. Being Earnest – Not That Important

Many nice guys fall into the 'earnest' category by accident, and it is a very hard hole to climb out of. To avoid being overly earnest, a few well timed self-deprecating jokes interspersed with some over the top claims will keep you well out of there, if you think it is a trap you could fall into. It comes down to self-awareness. Know how you are coming across.

7. Too Good To Be True

Now we have to be careful of being so fantastic that we tread on mythical ground. If your branding is too strong, it might make you seem a bit too good to be true. And mostly, if it seems too good to be true, people assume it is. You want to balance it out, so admitting to a humorous flaw is a good way around this. Nothing too deep (no mentions of your depression or overeating habit), and nothing that comes off as false modesty. If you can't think of a humorous flaw that doesn't include bodily/toilet/teenage humour, then try for something that will open up a conversation or allow for an invitation, such as 'I'm not a great cook, but would love to learn how to make Creme Brûlée.'

8. A Long Time Ago, In A Galaxy Far, Far Away

Any story that needs a prologue because it was so long ago will make your reader wonder why you haven't done anything recently. Maybe you did have a really exciting childhood, and perhaps a hint of that could be interesting. But you want to make sure it is clear that you also have a great life now, one that has space and interest for someone else.

9. Too Long

We will talk more about your summary's length in the next section, but here I want to mention summaries that are too long because the author hasn't taken the time to edit them properly. You want to make sure that EVERY word you write has a purpose, and that each idea is succinct. Keep in mind the lesson on pacing at the beginning of this section. Keep it short if you want to keep them excited and interested.

10. Too Short

On the other hand, even if you want fast pacing, you need to be careful of your profile is not too short. If there aren't enough details, people will feel you are hiding something, you are lazy, or incapable of using polysyllabic words. Use enough detail that someone feels they have a good grasp of your personality but definitely want to learn more… in person.

Try This Instead

The big list of negatives should help you steer clear of major pitfalls. Now, here are some tips to make your profile sparkle.

1. Please, Please, Please Be Positive

Even if life has treated your badly, killed your cat and left you living back with your parents, if you can turn this into a positive, it will be a lot more attractive. Things might have been bad, but they are going to get better from here on in, if only because you have such a great attitude. You are interested in online dating, and not at all self-conscious about it, because you know that there are some great people online, and you can't wait to meet them.

2. Try Putting In A Few Questions

Avoiding the too serious, 'Are you the one?' type questions, general questions about preferences and activity ideas will help start conversation. They get the reader engaged and thinking, and wanting to talk with you – and that's the whole point of your profile. You might be searching for the best dry Martini in town, and ask for any great suggestions... you never know where that could lead. Despite all the work you have done researching your target market and creating your brand, if your profile/contact email doesn't lead to a dialogue, you're not going to get anywhere.

3. Keep It Light

Similar to being positive, try to keep the mood light. Maybe over drinks you want to get into some deep and meaningful discussions, but don't drag someone who is just happily browsing into your philosophical musings on life. Try to work out what frame of mind they will be in while searching, and either match that or break it in an interesting and engaging way. Deep questions on philosophy or politics are usually not the way.

4. 250 Words.

I've read that 250 words is the standard length for advertising copy, as it gives just enough information while still keeping the reader's attention. This is something to keep in mind. However, another psychological study found that while longer profiles did turn off more readers, those who were compatible would read through and feel more firmly that they were a match. Giving someone the opportunity to realise they are not a match and someone else that they are a great match is not a bad thing. You really only want the good matches to contact you anyway.

A summary for any guys who are still a little lost and confused:

- Stick to your branding and focus on what your target market would want to hear, not trying to appeal to the broadest possible range.

- Use the skills of a writer to tell engaging stories and paint pictures that will last in the reader's mind and make them feel like they really know you.

- Be positive and self-aware.

- Being too short is a problem, but being too long is not a problem if you make the most of those words and allow someone who is compatible to get to know you.

Interests

I'm going to take a moment to talk about the interest list, because this can be quite difficult. Obviously the very nature of the question calls for you to list items. Unless you live for the next zombie TV series and are only looking for someone to share your nightly couch time with, don't list every series, movie, album and book you love. Instead, go through your enormous list and pick three from each category and say why you have chosen them. This turns it from a list into a chance to have a conversation. Try to show some diversity in your choices, and keep in mind names your target market might recognise. This does not mean putting in 'The Notebook' because you think all girls love it. That is just condescending. You need to explain why **you** love it, why it is one of only three you've listed.

Just one more thing before you can start drafting your profile, and it really is one of the most important aspects...

CHAPTER TWELVE

WHAT YOU ARE LOOKING FOR

Describing Your Ideal

If there is no separate category for it, the conclusion of every profile should include a description of what you are looking for in a partner, finished with a 'call to action', as those in the internet marketing world say.

First of all, there is no point having a general message that does not narrow down what you are looking for. Examples I've seen go along the lines of 'Contact me if you feel like it' or 'Contact me if you want to chat'. That is not inspiring, and it suggests you are desperate because you are not at all selective and would be happy with anything at all. Even if that were the case, it will say more about you than you want it to, and will detract from your overall profile and message. So don't be afraid to be specific.

When writing up what you are looking for, all the rules we have used for describing yourself still apply. It is important that the type of person you describe sounds attractive and interesting. This will cause women to want to be that person, and therefore encourage them to contact you. The thinking goes that if you reply, it validates that they are that interesting.

Most of the same 'don'ts' also still apply. You don't want to put out a shopping list. No girl thinks of themselves as a shopping list, and it makes you seem fussy. You also don't want to put anything in negative terms, because it either makes you look like a negative person, or suggests you have hang ups about these areas. Comments such as 'Don't message me if …' won't make other people want to message you more.

So, how do you write an attractive summary of your ideal woman? As I've said before, storytelling is always a great way to go. It's not the only way, but I'm a big fan. You want to create a picture that captures the essence of your ideal woman, is attractive, and has small details that will speak to your target market. For example, you might describe an ideal first meeting, or what your first date might be like, how you imagine they would spend Sunday morning.

(Just to let you know, this trick can also be used for your own self-summary section, so feel free to practice with it.)

For example:

If we met in a coffee shop, I would be attracted straight away by your smile and notice the fact you were reading a lonely planet guidebook for South America. I would feel we had something in common because you had a yoga mat next to you and were drinking green tea.

Or,

I'm looking for someone who loves slow Sunday mornings, enjoying a home cooked breakfast of buckwheat pancakes with organic maple syrup and fair-trade coffee. In the afternoon, we would work in the garden together digging the new veggie patch, before having late night discussions over red wine about politics and climate change.

These images should appeal to some people, but not to others. However, they are not negative, they don't say to everyone else 'You are not wanted, you are not good enough'. Instead, they have details that indicate what you are looking for. By stating 'fair-trade coffee', you are appealing to someone who is socially conscious. Other people won't feel offended because that is what you want, but won't feel like you are talking to them. Which is great, because you aren't. However, if telling it as a story is too intimidating, or beyond your writing skill, you can keep it as simple prose. Just remember to make it descriptive and positive.

Call To Action

Always remember to finish your profile with a 'call to action'. This is generally the 'Message me if...' I recommend describing your perfect person first, and then adding on the end a short and clear call to action. Once again, being vague is not in your favour. Saying 'Message me if you want to' is not going to stir many people to action. It also gives them no reason to do it, or any idea what to say if they do message you. Instead, you want something that is clear, enticing, and also makes it easy for them.

Some websites will have multiple different contacting options, so be specific about what you want them to do. Do you want them to message you, like you, add you to their favourites?

Then give them a reason to do so, something that would appeal to your target audience. If you really want to play this up, you can offer them something and then follow this up with a question or something that they can comment on. For example, you might say that they should contact you if they want to know the best coffee spots in town, then finish by asking how they would describe themselves in coffee terms. Would they be an espresso or a flat white? Why? This works best if the question gets them thinking about themselves (and who doesn't like thinking about themselves?) and gives them a chance to express that to you.

A good finish is like the conclusion of an essay or debate, and should make the person walk away still thinking about something you said. You want them to remember you, even if they don't contact you straight away. Though, ideally, you want them to read it and feel compelled to reply right there and then.

Finally, two things to be careful of if you haven't dated for a while. These come up in profiles quite a lot, in various forms, so I wanted to bring it to your attention just to help you steer clear.

Firstly, be careful that what you are specifying doesn't say more about you than it does about your partner. How you phrase your ideal person should make you sound like an intelligent, positive, appreciative person, not narrow-minded, bigoted, unrealistic and/or shallow. Even in this part you still want to maintain your branding and positive image.

Second, make sure you aren't listing something that you shouldn't expect in a romantic partner. While being single can be lonely, etc., being in a relationship won't magically fix everything. Particularly, please, please, please avoid even hinting that you think your partner will act as a therapist. If you are hoping to attract women by being needy, let me tell you now, this will fail.

PART FIVE
FINAL STEPS

CHAPTER THIRTEEN

POLISHING

Don't Skip This!

As a writer and an academic tutor I beg you: do not post unedited work anywhere, ever.

This applies doubly for online profiles. If this is important to you, and finding a great partner should be important, then do your future partner the courtesy of taking a few minutes to read through your whole profile and edit it.

Keep in mind that spelling and grammar are one of the biggest cues available through the written medium. You are judged on your mistakes because they are one of the easiest things to pick up on. These will make you seem either lazy or uneducated. Cues such as grammar, spelling and writing style are often seen as more meaningful about you as a person than your actual message. You will never turn someone off because your spelling is perfect, but you will definitely turn off a large proportion of people because your spelling is bad.

So, here are some quick and easy tips on editing.

1. Cut 10%. Okay, that's not a hard and fast rule, but I want you to go through and try to cut out as much as you can while still keeping the same meaning. Do you have superfluous words that add nothing to your message? The cleaner and sharper your writing, the clearer your message will be. Make sure that every word is fulfilling a vital purpose. Otherwise, kill it.

2. Sepll-Checker. Sounds stupid, but make sure there is a spell-checker wherever you are writing. You should be writing everything in a Word document (or similar), so that you can think about it, work on it, edit it etc. You should never be writing it directly onto the webpage, because it means you aren't taking long enough. Also, some browsers still don't have a spell-checker built in, so you would need to copy and paste it into a Word document anyway.

3. Read it aloud. Try to always read your work aloud. It is even better if you can get a friend to read it aloud, because then you will be able to hear where other people struggle with phrasing or meaning. If you have to explain to your friend that it should be read a certain way, then you have failed in your writing. You never get a chance to explain to your reader, so make sure you don't

need to. If you can't get someone to read it aloud to you, you can always try a text to speech feature where the computer reads it to you. Not as good, but it will highlight mistakes that you might have skimmed over yourself.

4. If you didn't get a friend to read it before, get them to do it now to make sure your profile says what you think it says. This is particularly important if your surveys shows you didn't have a great understanding of your unintentional cues.

5. Now, I want you to read it aloud in a stalker or pornstar voice. Is it offensive? Then change it. Is it creepy? Change it! No one is going to be doing you any favours online, so make it fool-proof. If it could be misinterpreted in any way, change it.

After you have done all that, it's finally, finally time to take it live!

CHAPTER FOURTEEN

MORE MARKET TESTING

Split Testing Time

Now that we have finally finished writing your profile, it's time to do some market testing! By this stage you should have polished your writing to perfection, and gotten your profile checked by friends to make sure you aren't giving off any unintended meanings. (The thing about unintended meanings is that you don't realise you are doing them! That's why you need to get someone else in to help.)

Even though we have put all this effort into making the perfect profile, what actually works for your target market is variable and unknown until you test it. Therefore, we are going to treat your profile as any company would a new product: we are going to do some market testing.

Big companies can afford to gather focus groups and get their opinions on the products and different features. If you know some people who are your target market but not actually available (friend's girlfriends/wives) you could ask them to comment on your profile. However, this is not very reliable as they know you, and would be influenced by their prior knowledge. Further, they might be nicer to you than a stranger would be because they know they don't really have to go out with you and/or don't want to hurt your feelings.

Enter split testing.

Split testing is simple. You create two versions of the same thing with a few key differences between the two. Remember in the branding exercise I said to come up with a few alternatives? Well, they come into play here. You take your profile information and change one or two bits. If you are happy with your branding, try small changes such as a different main photo or tagline. If you have a few different branding options, then changing one of your characteristics and include a new photo to support it. Then you put up one profile on one website, and the other profile on another website (or if you have more time, you can put one profile on a site and then a few weeks later try another profile on the same site and see if the changes attract a better response). You measure the results from each profile: do you get more contact? Do you get more replies to your contact? Are the people replying closer to your ideal? I recommend trying this on a large site where anyone can contact you rather than one of the matchmaking sites, which is a different ball game. Once you think you have close to the perfect description, but can't find the right person on the site, then open up accounts on other websites.

And you keep testing, and changing things, and improving your profile for as long as it takes to find what you are looking for.

It sounds simple, but you should definitely try it. It can be the little changes that make the difference between a good match contacting you or not.

Once you have all this working, then you need to keep updating your profile. As you do more exciting things, find out new interests, or learn new skills, these should all be included. And keep in mind that most sites display how frequently you login, so you want to keep coming back and checking things so you can stay at the top of the list. A lot of people won't contact someone who hasn't been online for a while. Make sure that's not you.

Yes, this is going to take a while, but don't you think it is fun? And just think of the great people you will meet along the way and how much you will learn about yourself (and others!).

CHAPTER FIFTEEN

WE HAVE CONTACT

How To Make Contact

We're getting to the gritty (yet exciting!) end of the process. How you make first contact or reply to someone else approaching you can make or break your chances. Each contact needs as much thought as the rest of your profile, and needs to continue and enhance your branding.

Here are some general tips on how to make the first contact.

1. Keep it short and light. The first contact is just to introduce yourself and spark her interest. It is not where you beg her to sleep with you, or bury her with your problems. Anything too long, and she will just skim it or

not read it at all. If it is short and positive, you will get a much better response rate.

2. Please make sure you have read her profile all the way through first! I have been contacted by guys who clearly have only looked at my photo and couldn't be bothered reading anything. This is insulting and immediately writes them off in my book. It is usually clear they haven't read my profile because they are asking completely irrelevant things. To make it clear you're not one of those guys, try to refer to one thing in her profile in your message.

3. No matter how perfect for you she sounds, if you are specifically not what she lists, think twice about messaging her. You need to think about why she would want to respond to you, not why you might be interested in her. If you can't find something in her profile for which you are a great match, move onto the next person.

4. Finish with a question. Remember, you are opening a dialogue, so you need to give her something she can actually reply to. This is something you need to do all the way through your email conversations. Always give her something to reply to, or she might not reply.

5. Be socially acceptable. You are entering into her personal space when you message her, and the same social rules apply as they would anywhere else. Don't try to attract attention by being offensive or confrontational. You

haven't earned the right to ask really personal questions, and even though you have read her profile, you still don't actually know anything about her. So please be a gentleman. (I'm sure you would be regardless.)

6. Be prepared to make the first move. A lot of women don't feel comfortable making the first move, even though they have signed up for online dating. However, don't be scared off if a girl contacts you. Accept her however she is, and let her approach or response teach you about her, and how she may want you to respond to her.

7. Hustle (as they say in the online world). After going through all this, you need to continue to be proactive. Aim to send a certain number of messages per week. This will get you noticed by other users, and for some sites will register you on their algorithms and put you higher in their search rankings. But make sure you don't contact too many people in one day – what if they all want a date that week?

8. Make each message unique. It should be tailored specifically to the person you are sending it to. It is pretty obvious if it is generic, and once again is just insulting. Even if you are sending out a few messages a day, you should always be interested in each individual person for some reason, so focus on that.

9. Maintain your grammar and spelling! It will set off alarm bells if your profile looks great, but then your

message is full of errors. It will suggest that your profile is fake.

10. Some sites you can send an electronic 'wink' (or some such) for free, but have to pay to send a message. If you really want to contact her, pay your money and send a proper message. If you just want to see if she will reply, send a wink but be prepared to follow it up with a real message. If you initiate contact, you should be the first one to pay to connect.

11. Try strong, positive, emotional words. The study by Rosen *et al.* (2008) found that messages with strong emotional words such as 'excited' and 'wonderful' had more positive impressions than those with weaker emotional words such as 'happy' and 'fine'. Just don't go over the top.

If you are not sure about your messages … keep split testing! Try wording your messages differently and see which gives you a better response. Keep track of the types of messages that get the best response, and see if you can improve on those.

Keep in mind that you won't always get a response. Don't take this personally; you don't know what is happening in their life, what bad experiences they are going through online, or what they are really looking for. It would be great if everyone responded, but it doesn't happen. I have to admit that I started off responding to everyone because I thought it was only polite. However, I then got a number of people trying to argue back why I should go out with them or being rude because I said I wasn't interested. So now I just don't respond. Don't let it eat your confidence – there are a lot of women out there who aren't right for you. The whole reason we're doing this is to find a gem who is.

PART SIX

CONCLUSION

Summary

We've looked at how psychology, internet marketing and writing can help you create a stronger and more persuasive profile. Now is just the beginning – like anything, the more you practice writing about yourself, the better you will get.

Every few months it is worthwhile going over your target market criteria and your branding to make sure you still are looking for the same things. Tastes change, and you might learn more about yourself and what you want after going on a number of dates.

And as you get more confident online, why not start looking a bit offline as well? There is a world of possibilities out there, waiting just for you.

Final Words

I have some final advice I want to give to those in particular who haven't dated a lot recently. Dating is like any skill, unless you keep practicing you tend to lose the touch. It is a Catch 22: the less you date, the less likely you are to get a date. Guys that don't date a lot tend to be shyer, have lower self-esteem (in this area), can have more negative beliefs and less social skills. These things will also affect your chances of maintaining a relationship if you do get past the first gatepost. Therefore, if you are serious about wanting a relationship, it is your responsibility to work out these issues. Someone else can't 'fix' these things for you.

There are profiles out there that try the whole 'I haven't dated for a long time', 'It's really hard for me', and 'Why won't someone love me?' angles. You need to realise this is not attractive. Never seek pity dates.

So what I want you to do is this:

1. Make sure your profile and communications are positive, no matter how bad you are feeling at the time.

2. Try other methods to combat some of these problems. This could be putting more active practice into your social skills, and taking yourself out of your comfort zone repeatedly and with purpose. This may even include seeing a counsellor to talk through some of it. These are great things to do before meeting the girl of your dreams.

3. Finally, when online, focus on the first steps. Just try to strike up conversations. Holding down a conversation for a few weeks with a girl might be better than anything you've done for a long time. Set yourself up for lots of little wins, rather than for big fails. If you can go

on a few dates, that would be great! Don't get upset if they just turn into friendships, because more friendships with females will help you to develop the social skills you need when you finally meet someone who could be more.

So get out there and have some fun!

REFERENCES

Ellison, N., Heino, R., and Gibbs, J., (Jan 2006), "Managing Impressions Online: Self-Presentation Process In The Online Dating Environment," *Journal of Computer-Mediated Communication*, 11/2, pp. 415-441.

Finkel, E. J., Eastwick, P. W., Karney, B. R., Reis, H. T., and Sprecher, S., (Jan 2012), "Online Dating: A Critical Analysis From the Perspective of Psychological Science," *Psychological Science in the Public Interest*, 13/1, pp. 3-66.

Fiore, A. T., and Donath, J. S., (2005), "Homophily in Online Dating: When Do You Like Someone Like Yourself?" *Extended Abstracts of Computer-Human Interaction*, pp. 1371-1374.

Fiore, A. T., Taylor, L.S., Mendelsohn, G.A., and Hearst, M.A., (2008), "Assessing Attractiveness in Online Dating Profiles," *Proceeding of the twenty-sixth annual SIGCHI conference on human factors in computing systems*, ACM Press, pp. 797-806.

133

Goffman, E., (1956), *The Presentation of Self in Everyday Life*, (New York: Doubleday).

Higgins, E. T., (1987), "Self-Descrepancy: A Theory Relating Self and Affect," *Psychological Review*, 94/3, pp. 319-340.

Joinson, A. N., (2001), "Self-disclosure in Computer-Mediated Communication: The Role of Self-Awareness and Visual Anonymity," *European Journal of Social Psychology*, 31/2, pp. 177–192.

Knox, D., Daniels, V., Sturdivant, L., and Zusman, M. E., (2001), "College Students Use of the Internet For Mate Selection," *College Student Journal*, 35, pp. 158-160.

Rosen, L. D., Cheever, N. A., Cummings, C., and Felt, J., (Sept. 2008), "The Impact of Emotionality and Self-Disclosure on Online Dating Versus Traditional Dating," *Computers in Human Behavior*, 24/5, pp. 2124-2157.

Walther, J. B., (1996), "Computer Mediated Communication: Impersonal, Interpersonal, and Hyperpersonal Interaction," *Communication Research*, 23/1, pp. 3-44.

Walther, J. B., Slovacek, C., and Tidwell, L. C., (2001), "Is A Picture Worth A Thousand Words?

Photographic Images in Long Term and Short Term Virtual Teams," *Communication Research,* 28/1, pp.105-134.

WANT MORE?

If you enjoyed reading this, check out some of my other works through www.100firstdrafts.com
I would also really appreciate a review on Amazon or Goodreads, so let me know what you think.

www.ingramcontent.com/pod-product-compliance
Lightning Source LLC
Chambersburg PA
CBHW050350280326
41933CB00010BA/1400